J.K. ROWLING

Other titles in the Greenhaven Press Literary Companion to Contemporary Authors series:

Tom Clancy
Michael Crichton
John Grisham
Stephen King

The Greenhaven Press
LITERARY COMPANION
to Contemporary Authors

READINGS ON

J.K. ROWLING

Gary Wiener, *Book Editor*

Daniel Leone, *President*
Bonnie Szumski, *Publisher*
Scott Barbour, *Managing Editor*

GREENHAVEN
PRESS ®

THOMSON

———————*———————
™
GALE

San Diego • Detroit • New York • San Francisco • Cleveland
New Haven, Conn. • Waterville, Maine • London • Munich

© 2003 by Greenhaven Press. Greenhaven Press is an imprint of The Gale Group, Inc., a division of Thomson Learning, Inc.

Greenhaven® and Thomson Learning™ are trademarks used herein under license.

For more information, contact
Greenhaven Press
27500 Drake Rd.
Farmington Hills, MI 48331-3535
Or you can visit our Internet site at http://www.gale.com

Cover credit: © Murdo Macleod/CORBIS

LIBRARY OF CONGRESS CATALOGING-IN-PUBLICATION DATA

Readings on J.K. Rowling / Gary Wiener, book editor.
    p. cm. — (The Greenhaven Press literary companion to contemporary authors)
    Includes bibliographical references and index.
    ISBN 0-7377-1668-1 (lib. : alk. paper) — ISBN 0-7377-1669-X (pbk. : alk. paper)
    1. Rowling, J.K.—Criticism and interpretation. 2. Children's stories, English—History and criticism. 3. Fantasy fiction, English—History and criticism.
    4. Rowling, J.K.—Characters—Harry Potter. 5. Potter, Harry (Fictitious character)
    6. Wizards in literature. 7. Magic in literature. I. Wiener, Gary. II. Series.
    PR6068.O93Z845 2003
    823'.914—dc21   2003040760

Printed in the United States of America

Contents

Chapter 1: J.K. Rowling and Her Work

Written to coincide with the publication of the third
Harry Potter novel, *Harry Potter and the Prisoner of
Azkaban,* this viewpoint introduces the books to those
unfamiliar with the *Harry Potter* phenomenon. The
article establishes the incredible popularity of the novels, offers a brief biography of Rowling, and examines
how she came to write the world's most popular children's novels.

Jim Trelease places the *Harry Potter* books within the
tradition of series books, long a favorite genre among
children. While some adults see series books as a waste
of time for young people, who may be corrupted by
their lack of moral content, Trelease contends that
these books provide an important gateway through
which young people can experience the joys of reading.

J.K. Rowling has a love affair with quirky words and
names, and this viewpoint explores the meanings and
origins of the language of the *Harry Potter* books. For
example, the word *Muggle* is dissected, as are numerous
character and place names. Rowling's unique language
is the key to her wonderful world of wizardry.

Chapter 2: *Harry Potter's* Place in Literature

Stone on two fronts: literary and social. The book can be appropriately placed in the British children's fantasy novel tradition alongside works by renowned British authors Lewis Carroll and C.S. Lewis. Regarding stereotypes in the novel, it must be remembered that *Harry Potter* is fantasy and does not attempt to tackle social evils in the manner of contemporary realistic fiction.

Chapter 3: Critical Response to *Harry Potter*

sensical reason. Reading *Harry Potter* books is an enjoyable experience for young people, and that should be reason enough for letting young people read them.

FOREWORD

Contemporary authors who earn millions of dollars writing best-sellers often face criticism that their work cannot be taken seriously as literature. For example, throughout most of his career, horror writer Stephen King has been dismissed by literary critics as a "hack" who writes grisly tales that appeal to the popular taste of the masses. Similarly, the extremely popular Harry Potter books by J.K. Rowling have been criticized as a clever marketing phenomenon that lack the imagination and depth of classic works of literature. Whether these accusations are accurate, however, remains debatable. As romance novelist Jayne Ann Krentz has pointed out:

> Popular fiction has been around forever but rarely has it been viewed as important in and of itself. Rarely have we acknowledged that it has a crucial place in culture. . . . The truth is, popular fiction—mysteries, science fiction, sword and sorcery, fantasy, glitz, romance, historical saga, horror, techno-thrillers, legal thrillers, forensic medical thrillers, serial killer thrillers, westerns, etc.—popular fiction is its own thing. It stands on its own. It draws its power from the ancient heroic traditions of storytelling—not modern angst. It is important, even if it is entertaining.

Although its importance often goes unrecognized, popular fiction has the power to reach millions of readers and to thus influence culture and society. The medium has the potential to shape culture because of the large and far-flung audience that is drawn to read these works. As a result of their large readership, contemporary authors have a unique venue in which to reflect and explore the social and political issues that they find important. Far from being mere escapist fiction, their works often address topics that challenge readers to consider their perspectives on current and universal themes. For example, Michael Crichton's novel *Jurassic Park*, while an entertaining if disturbing story about what could happen if dinosaurs roamed the planet today, also explores the potential negative consequences of scientific advances and the ethical issues of DNA experimentation. Similarly, in his 1994 novel *Disclosure*, Crichton tells the story of a man who suffers predatory sexual harassment by his female supervisor. By reversing the expected genders of the victim and aggressor, Crichton added fuel to the debate over sexual politics in the workplace.

Some works of fiction are compelling and popular because they address specific concerns that are prevalent in a culture at a given time. For example, John Grisham has written numerous novels about the theme of corruption in America's oldest legal and business institutions. In books such as *The Firm* and *The Pelican Brief*, courageous though sometimes naive individuals must confront established, authoritarian systems at great personal danger in order to bring the truth to light. Written at a time when government and corporate scandals dominated the headlines, his novels reflect a faith in the power of the individual to achieve justice.

In an era when 98 percent of American households have a television and annual video sales outnumber book sales, it is impossible to ignore the fact that popular fiction also inspires people to read. The Harry Potter stories have been enormously popular with both adults and children, setting records on the *New York Times* best-seller lists. Stephen King's books, which have never gone out of print, frequently occupy four to five shelves in bookstores and libraries. Although literary critics may find fault with some works of popular fiction, record numbers of people are finding value in reading these contemporary authors whose stories hold meaning for them and which shape popular culture.

Greenhaven Press's Literary Companion to Contemporary Authors series is designed to provide an introduction to the works of modern authors. Each volume profiles a different author. A biographical essay sets the stage by tracing the author's life and career. Next, each anthology in the series contains a varied selection of essays that express diverse views on the author under discussion. A concise introduction that presents the contributing writers' main themes and insights accompanies each selection. Essays, profiles, and reviews offer in-depth biographical information, analysis of the author's predominant themes, and literary analysis of the author's trademark books. In addition, primary sources such as interviews and the author's own essays and writings are included wherever possible. A comprehensive index and an annotated table of contents help readers quickly locate material of interest. In order to facilitate further research, each title includes a bibliography of the author's works and books about the author's writing and life. These features make Greenhaven Press's Literary Companion to Contemporary Authors series ideal for readers interested in literary analysis on the world's modern authors and works.

INTRODUCTION

There are some books—very few—that transcend their place as works of literature, assume a life of their own, and become a part of larger cultural forces. Miguel de Cervantes's *Don Quixote,* Jonathan Swift's *Gulliver's Travels,* Harriet Beecher Stowe's *Uncle Tom's Cabin,* George Orwell's *1984,* and Joseph Heller's *Catch-22* all altered people's perceptions and introduced new words into everyday English usage. It may be premature to place the *Harry Potter* series among these literary masterworks, although any of *Harry Potter*'s millions of fans might disagree. Certainly, the series' astonishing sales figures suggest that the *Harry Potter* books have made reading fashionable for youngsters once again. Only time will tell whether *Harry Potter* will permanently restore the magic of reading for a generation raised on video games and music videos.

Harry Potter is more than just a fictional character or a book series. J.K. Rowling's creation is a full-fledged sensation that has become part of popular culture. There are now *Harry Potter* collector's cards, shampoos, candies, action figurines, video games, Christmas ornaments, and more. The first *Harry Potter* movie, released in fall 2001, generated huge ticket sales worldwide. As columnist George Will has suggested, *Harry Potter* is "the most eagerly awaited British export since the Beatles." Indeed, the publication of each new volume in the *Harry Potter* series is greeted by adoring fans in a way not seen since the Beatles were in their heyday. So eager is the reading public to see new *Harry Potter* adventures that when an obviously fraudulent fifth installment, titled *Harry Potter and Leopard Walk Up to Dragon,* came out in

12

China, readers there came out in droves to buy copies.

What is it about the *Harry Potter* series that has so galvanized a young reading public's attention on a worldwide scale? The books, as many critics have noted, are not wholly original: They combine elements of the English fantasy novel, made internationally famous by C.S. Lewis and J.R.R. Tolkien, with elements of the boarding school novel, another established English genre. What brings the series alive is what the critics call verisimilitude, by which Rowling invents an entire magical society that seems real. This society, effectively hidden from everyday people, or Muggles, has its own literature, its own treats (for example, Bertie Bott's Every Flavor Beans), its own transportation system (chiefly brooms), and, especially, its own sport (Quidditch). So convincingly does Rowling portray this fantasy world that readers everywhere can empathize with Harry and his friends as they struggle against evil.

As is often the case with a cultural phenomenon, the unprecedented success of *Harry Potter* has created a critical backlash. As the first three *Harry Potter* books began to monopolize the top spots on the *New York Times* best-seller list in a way that no series has done before, a number of prominent critics, Harold Bloom and William Safire among them, insisted that *Harry Potter* was not a worthy successor to great nineteenth-century works such as *Alice in Wonderland* or *Huckleberry Finn.* Nor, said critics, could the *Harry Potter* series rival the twentieth-century fantasy books to which it was most often compared, C.S. Lewis's *Narnia* series or J.R.R. Tolkien's *Lord of the Rings* trilogy. The *New York Times* even went to the remarkable length of establishing a separate children's best-seller list so that the *Harry Potter* novels would no longer dominate the ranks of adult fiction. Rarely has a cultural institution like a leading newspaper actually changed its rules in response to a new phenomenon. But the cultural force of *Harry Potter* was undeniable, and nothing that even the most influential literary critics could say against the books, from accusations that they are clichéd to charges of a stilted writing style, could dampen readers' enthusiasm for Rowling's books.

J.K. Rowling has indicated that she will write seven *Harry Potter* novels and that they will be progressively more complex. A series that began with a light comedic touch in the first volume has darkened considerably in tone in the middle volumes. Rowling has clearly struggled in her attempts to treat the battle between archetypes of good and evil in a serious way. This difficulty caused the fifth book in the series, which Rowling's publisher is thought to have planned to release in the summer of 2001, to be delayed considerably. Rowling's success with the first four volumes has created for the author a challenge rivaled only by the struggle of Harry Potter versus Voldemort and his minions, as she labors to conclude the series in a fashion that lives up to its early promise. Moreover, she must do so before a worldwide audience. For *Harry Potter* fans everywhere, it will be fascinating to witness how J.K. Rowling and her young wizard conclude their parallel journeys.

J.K. Rowling: A Biography

Perhaps the only story more improbable than the adventures of a teenage wizard named Harry Potter is the life story of Harry's creator, J.K. Rowling. In the space of just a few years, she was almost magically transformed from an unknown who had never published even a short story to the most popular writer in the world. The odds against an unknown writer landing a book contract in the first place are daunting. But the odds against such a writer achieving worldwide success are astronomical. Yet J.K. Rowling beat those odds, and at the dawn of the twenty-first century, Rowling's adventures of Harry Potter outsell books by such popular authors as Stephen King, John Grisham, and Tom Clancy.

Childhood

The extraordinary story of J.K. Rowling (or Joanne, as she was named by her parents) began in an ordinary way. Joanne's parents, Peter and Ann Rowling, met in King's Cross Station in London, while they were on their way to Scotland, in the early 1960s. Peter was traveling to join the Royal Navy and Ann to become a Wren (part of the Women's Royal Naval Service). Years later, Rowling would celebrate this meeting by including King's Cross Station in the *Harry Potter* books as the magical place where the train for Hogwarts leaves from platform 9¾.

Peter and Ann's relationship quickly deepened. At the same time, as their attachment to one another was growing, both Peter and Ann were becoming disenchanted with the Royal Navy and decided to return to civilian life together. Although they were both from London, the young couple desired a small-town existence. And so they came to the town of Yate, near the city of Bristol in southwest England. Peter Rowling took a job in the engineering field, as an apprentice on the production line at the Bristol Siddeley factory, where aircraft engines were built.

By the time of their marriage on March 14, 1965, Ann was five months' pregnant. Joanne Kathleen Rowling was born on July 31, 1965. As she grew, she proved to be a bright, inquisitive child who loved hearing her parents read to her. This continual exposure to literature had a profound effect on Joanne, and she began to invent her own stories at a young age. When her younger sister, Di, was born in 1967, Joanne had a playmate and a future audience.

By the late 1960s, the Rowlings decided that the ever-expanding Yate no longer offered the rural community life they desired, and so they moved to Winterbourne, a small town on the other side of the city of Bristol. By 1971, after a series of takeovers, the Bristol Siddeley factory where Peter worked was merged into the Rolls Royce company. Peter Rowling was a dedicated and hardworking employee who soon began to work his way up into management.

At the age of six, Joanne was already inventing tales about a rabbit that she simply called Rabbit and a giant bee named Miss Bee. She kept Di entertained with these stories. It was at this young age that Joanne Rowling first knew what she wanted to do in life. "Ever since Rabbit and Miss Bee, I knew I wanted to be a writer," she later said. "I cannot overstate how much I wanted that. But I would rarely tell anyone so."

Joanne's imagination and creativity did not go unnoticed by neighbors. In Winterbourne, Joanne and Di had many friends. Among these friends were a brother and sister named Ian and Vicki Potter. Ian remembers that Joanne's favorite game was playing witches and wizards. "The children were forever pinching [taking] the brooms from the garage to use as broomsticks," recalls Ruby Potter, Ian's and Vicki's mother. "Joanne was always in charge, always the leader."

In 1974 the family moved once again, to Tutshill in South Wales. The location would one day be reflected in Rowling's work. Tutshill, Rowling notes, "was dominated by a castle on a cliff, which might explain a lot." In Tutshill, Joanne got off to a rough start at her new school because she was behind in mathematics. But it did not take her long to impress her new teacher with her intelligence and willingness to work hard.

Joanne read constantly during this time, counting among her favorite works Elizabeth Goudge's *The Little White Horse,* Paul Gallico's *Manxmouse,* and tellingly, C.S. Lewis's *Narnia* books, a fantasy series about young boys and girls who step through a bedroom closet into another world. Today, when young people ask Rowling for advice on becoming a writer, her response is not hard to predict. "The most important thing is to read as much as you can, like I did," she says. "It will give you an understanding of what makes good writing and it will enlarge your vocabulary. And it's a lot of fun!"

Reading became a driving force in young Joanne's life. By the age of nine, Joanne Rowling was already reading books aimed at much older readers. For example, she read Ian Fleming's *James Bond* novels and fell in love with the works of nineteenth-century novelist Jane Austen. "Jane Austen is my favorite author, ever," Rowling has said. Another favorite was Jessica Mitford, a feminist who often wrote about human rights. Mitford's book *Hons and Rebels,* which Joanne read at fourteen, had a profound effect on the young girl. Joanne, who rarely disobeyed her parents or other adults, admired the rebellious qualities that came through in the book. "[Mitford] had tremendous moral courage and did some physically brave things as a human rights activist," Rowling has said, acknowledging that she "wished she had the nerve" to stand up for herself as Mitford had.

Joanne often felt awkward during her early teens. Of this period in her life, she would later say, "I think I was always very insecure, a real worrier, but I would put on a show of confidence to mask it. I might just have been a tiny bit

Hermione-ish." Joanne would entertain her friends by telling them tales she had invented. Some of these stories Rowling committed to paper, but most she kept in her head. As Joanne moved through her middle and high school years at Wyedean Comprehensive, she began to gain confidence in herself. "I did relax as I got older which was a good thing, although I was still—and am still—a worrier." By her senior year, Joanne was named head girl, an honorary position reserved for a top student. She graduated from Wyedean Comprehensive with top honors.

SEARCHING FOR A CAREER

Even though she had been an outstanding student, Rowling's future was unclear. She desired, as she had always done, to become a writer. But despite having written stories, the next step, seeking publication, was not easy for her. Rowling, was fearful of submitting her work to the scrutiny of others, and these fears kept her from sending her work out to magazines for publication.

Meanwhile, Rowling made plans to continue her education, applying to the prestigious Oxford University in England. Despite her excellent grades, she did not get accepted into this highly selective university. Rowling's parents believed that because their daughter had shown a particular talent for language and literature, she had a future as a bilingual legal secretary. For this reason they sent her to Exeter University, where she pursued a degree in modern languages with a concentration in French. Rowling attended Exeter for four years, including one year that she spent teaching English in Paris. She made many friends at Exeter and enjoyed her time there. But surprisingly for a student of her abilities, her grades were only average. In later years she would observe of her time at Exeter, "I don't think I worked as hard as I could have." During her time at Exeter she continued to write, even working on a novel, although she abandoned the project before it was completed.

After graduating from college in 1987, Rowling moved to London, where she worked for the human rights group Amnesty International as a researcher and bilingual secretary. The work bored her, however. The only thing she enjoyed about her job was the hours it afforded her at a computer, where, in her spare time, she could clandestinely type up the stories she was inventing. Rowling continued to find the work at Amnesty International boring, and over the next few years she held a succession of other secretarial jobs.

In June 1990, she considered moving to Manchester because an old boyfriend had gotten in touch with her and asked to see her again. One day, after spending the weekend in Manchester looking for a flat [apartment], she rode the train back to her London home. During this ride, the train broke down and was delayed for four long hours. As she waited, Rowling had a brainstorm in the form of an idea for a new book. "I have never felt such a huge rush of excitement," she would later say. "I knew immediately that this was going to be such fun to write. I didn't know then that it was going to be a book for children—I just knew that I had this boy, Harry. During that journey I also discovered Ron, Nearly Headless Nick, Hagrid, and Peeves." But with all of this brilliant information "careering round my head," Rowling made an unfortunate discovery: She had no pen that worked. She was forced to wait until she was able to return home before committing her idea to paper. But once back in her flat, Rowling wrote down everything she had imagined during that train ride.

The months that followed Rowling's brainstorm were among the most difficult of her life. She moved to Manchester as planned, taking a job with the Chamber of Commerce there, but was soon laid off. During this period, an even more traumatic event occurred. Rowling's mother, who had long been ill with multiple sclerosis, succumbed to the crippling disease at the age of only forty-five. Once again, Rowling was at a crossroads: She was out of work and depressed over her mother's death. Adding to her distress, her relationship with her boyfriend had soured. "It was a nightmare period," Rowling later told an interviewer. But she still had Harry Potter, and it was her work on his story that got her through.

PORTUGAL, MARRIAGE, AND MOTHERHOOD

A new job soon offered Rowling the chance to put some of her difficulties behind her. In September 1990 she accepted a position in Portugal as a teacher of English as a second language. "I knew that I'd enjoyed teaching English as a foreign language in Paris and I thought to myself, how would it be if I went abroad, did some teaching, took my manuscript, had some sun," she later said in explanation of her decision to make such a move. Rowling took a job in the town of Oporto in northern Portugal. At first, living in a foreign country intimidated her, but as she grew into her job and accustomed herself to the warmth of a southern climate, she felt more comfortable and confident. Her teaching duties, which entailed working with students from ages eight to sixty-two, occupied her afternoons and evenings. But she had the luxury of spending her mornings on her burgeoning novel about a young wizard.

Rowling had been living in Portugal for six months when she met her future husband, a journalist named Jorge Arantes. Both Rowling and Arantes were avid readers and writers, and their common interests spawned a friendship that quickly deepened. They were married on October 16, 1992. A year later, in 1993, Rowling gave birth to a daughter, Jessica, named after the writer who had so impressed her as a young girl, Jessica Mitford. "That was," Rowling says, "the best moment of my life." By this time, Rowling had completed and polished the first three chapters of the book she titled *Harry Potter and the Philosopher's Stone*. "The rest of the book was in rough draft."

Not long after the birth of Jessica, it became clear in Rowling's mind "that my marriage wasn't working." She and Jorge engaged in bitter arguments, and some of his actions bordered on physical abuse. Rowling decided to take her baby and return to Britain in November 1993. Because her sister and her best friend lived in Edinburgh, Scotland, that is where Rowling settled after she left Portugal. "I felt that Edinburgh was the kind of city in which I wanted to bring up my child," she has said. "Pretty soon I made some good friends. Maybe it was my Scottish blood calling me home."

HARRY POTTER COMES OF AGE

Rowling may have felt at home in Scotland, but life as an unemployed single mother was anything but easy. She could not afford to devote too much time to *Harry Potter* because she needed to support herself and Jessica. Rowling applied for the British equivalent of welfare, and survived during this period on a combination of just over one hundred dollars per month from the government and money borrowed from friends. Living on "the dole" made Rowling feel "humiliated and worthless," but there was no other way for her to make ends meet. In late 1994 she found work as a secretary, but learned that she could not earn more than twenty dollars a week and still collect her government benefits.

Many myths have sprung up about this period, myths that Rowling herself has sought to dispel. "A lot of rubbish has been written," she says about those who made up details of her life to fit their own image of a struggling writer. "Not necessarily malicious rubbish . . . but things get exaggerated and distorted." One such exaggeration was that Rowling was so poor that she had to write portions of the first *Harry Potter* book on paper napkins. Rowling has dispelled this rumor, saying,

> It wasn't enough that I was a penniless single mother, which was true. I had to write on napkins because I couldn't afford paper. . . . Let's not exaggerate here. Let's not pretend I had to write on napkins, because I didn't. They started adding little bits and pieces that just weren't necessary, because the stark reality was bad enough.

Another common misconception Rowling is quick to correct concerned her apartment in Edinburgh. "I did not write in cafes to escape my unheated flat," she says, "because I am not *stupid* enough to rent an unheated flat in Edinburgh in mid-winter—It had heat." In fact, Rowling has stated for the record that the reason she wrote in cafés was because of the sleeping habits of baby Jessica. In order to get Jessica to take a nap so that Rowling could concentrate on writing, she had to stroll around town pushing the baby carriage. The movement put Jessica to sleep, and Rowling would then head for the nearest café, take out her pen and paper, and continue her book.

Having fled from a failed marriage, lost her mother, and lost as well a series of teaching and secretarial jobs, Rowling was aimless in everything but her devotion to her *Harry Potter* manuscript. If not for that one pursuit, Rowling might have been easily viewed as a ne'er-do-well, a person who just cannot make it on her own. But there was always the manuscript. And throughout this period, Rowling was always at work on it. Writing the book did make demands on the single mother, and there were clearly sacrifices. Of her Edinburgh flat, she says, "Everything was very, very dilapidated, and always filthy, which wasn't the flat's fault, it was my fault. Because people always say, 'How did you do it? How did you raise a baby and write a book?' And the answer is I didn't do housework for four years."

As trying as these years in Edinburgh were, Rowling would later say that they had little influence on the plot of her book. "So much of *Harry Potter and the Sorcerer's Stone* was written and planned before I found myself a single mother that I don't think my experiences at that time directly influenced the plot or characters," she says. "I think the only event in my own life that changed the direction of 'Harry Potter' was the death of my mother. I only fully realized upon re-reading the book how many of my own feelings about losing my mother I had given Harry."

It took Rowling five years from that initial brainstorm in

the train from Manchester to London before she finished *Harry Potter and the Philosopher's Stone* (called *Harry Potter and the Sorcerer's Stone* in America). During that period, she generated a massive amount of material, "far more," she says, "than would ever find its way into the book." For the first chapter alone, she claims, she wrote fifteen different versions before settling on one that met her own high standards. In 1996, once she had completed the draft of the novel, Rowling typed the entire story on a manual typewriter. *Harry Potter* was finally ready to confront the world.

HARRY POTTER FINDS A PUBLISHER

But *Harry Potter and the Philosopher's Stone* was not published immediately. After all, Rowling was an unpublished writer, and, as such, was unlikely to be taken seriously by a major publisher. For this reason, her first step was to find a literary agent who would act as her representative. Agents, however, were also wary of an unknown writer, and the first agent she sent the manuscript to declined to work with her. But fortunately for Rowling, the second agent she tried, Christopher Little, agreed to represent her.

Again, success did not occur overnight. Though Little pitched the book to all of the major publishing houses in England, it was continually rejected. These publishers indicated that *Harry Potter* was too long for a children's novel. They also noted that having Harry attend a boarding school would be considered inappropriate in an age when parents were being urged to take responsibility for their children and most students lived at home while attending school.

In 1997, after a year's effort by Christopher Little, *Harry Potter and the Philosopher's Stone* was purchased by Bloomsbury Press, a reputable publishing company that had been founded in 1986. Bloomsbury paid a modest twenty-five hundred British pounds (or approximately four thousand dollars) for the book. Barry Cunningham, the Bloomsbury editor who accepted *Harry Potter*, laughs when he thinks about all of the publishers who could have easily purchased what would become the most popular books in the world before he did, but chose to pass. "It's a little like turning down the Beatles, isn't it?" he says.

Rowling was ecstatic over having her book accepted. Recalling her feelings at the birth of her daughter, she later said that news of the acceptance of her first novel was "the second best moment of my life." Looking back, Rowling claims that "Nothing since has come anywhere close to the fact that I was actually going to be published."

With publication of *Harry Potter and the Philosopher's Stone* now assured, Christopher Little suggested that Rowling adopt the initials "J.K." instead of using her first name. Having researched the effect of authors' names on book sales, he had learned that a female writer's name might alienate the young males whom he believed were the most likely readers of the novel. Thus was the author "J.K. Rowling" born.

RICH AND FAMOUS

Early in the first book in the *Harry Potter* series, Hagrid tells Harry, "You're famous." But if anyone had told Rowling that this scene would become reality and that the name Harry Potter would become as well known as that of Michael Jordan or Princess Di, she would have told them that they were crazy. And yet, as all the world knows, that is precisely what happened.

Harry Potter and the Philosopher's Stone finally appeared in English bookstores in June 1997. Eight days later, the rights to publish the novel in America were auctioned off. Scholastic Books, a leading publisher of children's literature in the United States, bought the American rights for $105,000, a figure completely unheard of for a first book by a children's author. One alteration that Scholastic insisted on was that the title be changed to *Harry Potter and the Sorcerer's Stone,* because "Philosopher's Stone" was deemed too abstract for American readers.

The sale of the American rights to her novel changed Rowling's life dramatically. Rowling knew that children's authors rarely made enough money to support themselves by writing alone, and so she had taken a job teaching French in order to support herself and Jessica. However, the money she received for her book's American rights gave Rowling the security she needed to devote herself to writing full-time.

In an article titled "Why I Paid So Much for a Children's Book" published in October 1999 in the *New York Times,* Scholastic's editorial director, Arthur A. Levine, stated what drew him to *Harry Potter:*

> The thing I loved the most about reading *Harry Potter* is the idea of growing up unappreciated, feeling outcast and then this great satisfaction of being discovered. That is the fantasy of every person who grows up feeling marginalized in any way. Along with the imagination and the wonderful writing, that's the emotional connection that drew me to the book.

Bloomsbury had released *Harry Potter and the Philosopher's Stone* in England on June 26, 1997, and though sales were, according to the publisher, "surprisingly good," and the book garnered good reviews by critics, there was, Rowling later recalled, "no great fanfare." Still, during this period, Rowling started to receive her first fan mail. "I remember my first ever fan letter," she says. "It began, 'Dear Sir. . . .'"

Harry Potter and the Philosopher's Stone not only proved a solid hit with the book-buying public in England but won numerous literary prizes as well, including the Nestle Smarties Book Prize, the Federation of Children's Books Group Award, and the British Book Awards Children's Book of the Year. These awards generated additional sales. By 1998, *Harry Potter and the Philosopher's Stone* had sold a half-million copies. Then, in August 1998, Scholastic released the book in America, and sales boomed. Rowling's decision to become a full-time writer seemed well justified.

This decision to devote herself solely to writing brought with it both fears and joys. Rowling was working on her second novel, *Harry Potter and the Chamber of Secrets*, but was concerned that it would not be as well received as her first one. And ever the perfectionist, she found it "incredibly hard to finish." She did complete this second installment in the series in time to meet her publisher's deadline, but she then took it back for six weeks in order to make changes until she was completely satisfied with the manuscript.

As successive *Harry Potter* books were released, J.K. Rowling saw her renown grow right along with Harry's. It was on her second tour of America, to promote the third installment, *Harry Potter and the Prisoner of Azkaban*, that Rowling began to notice Potter hysteria kick in. "On my previous tour," she recalled, "the greatest number of people at an event was probably about one hundred. My second tour began in Boston. As we were driving up to the bookshop I saw a massive queue [line] snaking along two blocks." When she asked the publisher's representative who was riding in the car with her if there was a sale nearby, the representative told Rowling that the line was for her. "It was the most extraordinary experience," Rowling said.

The release of the fourth novel in the series, the lengthy *Harry Potter and the Goblet of Fire*, sparked *Harry Potter* celebrations in bookstores across America. Many stores opened their doors at midnight so that clamoring fans could obtain a copy of the book in the very first minutes it was available. *Harry Potter* mania had reached a fever pitch. Despite its length and its complicated plot, *Harry Potter and the Goblet of Fire* shot to the top of the *New York Times* best-seller list and remained there for many weeks.

Rowling's success alleviated some worries. For example, she will never have to worry about money again. As of 2001, Rowling was reportedly worth $100 million, and she owns mansions in both Edinburgh and London. On the other hand, Rowling's fame has brought an enormous number of requests for interviews, book readings, charity donations, speeches, television appearances, and the like. Fulfilling such requests means adhering to a grueling schedule and, most important, cuts into her valuable writing time.

Personal commitments also make demands on time that Rowling might otherwise spend writing. On December 26, 2001, the thirty-six-year-old author married Neil Murray, a thirty-year-old doctor whom she met at a mutual friend's house in Edinburgh.

THE FUTURE OF *HARRY POTTER*

Rowling's enormous success has allowed her to indulge her interest in charity work, which led her to produce two slim books, *Fantastic Beasts and Where to Find Them* and *Quidditch Through the Ages*, which were released following the publication of *Harry Potter and the Goblet of Fire*. These volumes are purported textbooks studied by Harry Potter at Hogwarts, and come complete with marginal notes, scribbles, and doodles in Harry's own hand. Money from the sales of these books went to Comic Relief, an organization committed to fighting poverty and social injustice in the United Kingdom and the poorest countries in the world.

Such pursuits, however noble, have distracted Rowling from her work on the fifth book of the *Harry Potter* series, *Harry Potter and the Order of the Phoenix*. Once *Harry Potter and the Goblet of Fire* hit the bookshelves in August 2000, there was much speculation that the fifth book would arrive in 2001. When that date passed without the publication of a new *Harry Potter* novel, rumors circulated that Rowling was suffering from writer's block and could not complete the book. In a letter to the *Scotsman* newspaper, Rowling denied this allegation, stating that neither she nor her publisher, Bloomsbury, had ever promised that the fifth book would appear in 2001. Rowling added, "I made it clear last summer [in 2000] that I wanted to take the time to make sure that book five was not dashed off to meet a deadline, but was completed to my full satisfaction as its predecessors have been, as I was committed to producing two additional books for Comic Relief this year."

Rowling has insisted all along that there will be seven *Harry Potter* novels, which will take the hero from age eleven through high school graduation. She has no doubts that she will be able to finish the series "if only for myself." In a December 2001 interview with the British Broadcasting Corporation (BBC), J.K. Rowling revealed that she had already written the last chapter of the final *Harry Potter* book. She cautions readers that some of the boy wizard's adventures to come will make for distressing reading. The BBC program shows Rowling holding a yellow folder containing the final chapter of the series to the camera and saying, "This is it, and I'm not opening it for obvious reasons." She adds, "This really wraps everything, it's the epilogue and I basically say what happens to everyone after they leave school, those who survive—because there are deaths, more deaths coming. . . . There's at least one death that's going to be horrible to write."

Now that the books have been published in approximately forty languages and Harry Potter is a household name, one thing is for sure: Whatever adventures J.K. Rowling dreams up for her boy wizard, the world will be watching.

CHAPTER 1

J.K. Rowling and Her Work

READINGS ON

J.K. ROWLING

A *Harry Potter* Primer

Paul Gray

This article, published in *Time* magazine just after the publication of the third *Harry Potter* novel, *Harry Potter and the Prisoner of Azkaban*, attempts to explain the *Harry Potter* phenomenon to those who are not in the know. Cleverly beginning with a quiz on how to tell if you are a *Muggle*, the piece goes on to explain the rampant popularity of the first three *Potter* novels by asserting that Rowling "knows how to feed the desire not just to hear or read a story but to live it as well." Author Paul Gray also touches on Rowling's biography and shows how the press made Rowling's own life into an intriguing story in its own right. The article concludes with speculation about the remaining books in the series and the [at the time] upcoming movie version of *Harry Potter and the Sorcerer's Stone*. Gray notes, at the end, how in this age of technological wonders, the *Potter* novels use no technology, instead relying on old-fashioned magic.

First of all, for the uninitiated, here are three surefire, clinically tested signs that you are a Muggle:

1) You spot a boy or girl whose forehead is emblazoned with a paste-on tattoo in the shape of a purple lightning bolt and have no idea what you are seeing.

2) You still believe reading is a lost art, especially among the young, and books have been rendered obsolete in our electronic, hot-wired age.

3) You don't know what a Muggle is.

Fortunately, such ignorance has become almost ridiculously easy to remedy. Simply place yourself in the vicinity of a child,

Paul Gray, "Wild About Harry," *Time*, September 20, 1999, pp. 67–72. Copyright © 1999 by Time, Inc. Reproduced by permission.

just about any child, anywhere, and say the magic words Harry Potter. If, for instance, you utter this charm to Anna Hinkley, 9, a third-grader in Santa Monica, Calif., here is what you will learn: "What happens in the first book, Harry discovers that he's a wizard, and he's going to a school called Hogwarts School of Witchcraft and Wizardry. At the station he meets a boy named Ron, who's also going to Hogwarts. And on the train, they meet a girl named Hermione. . . ." Given enough time, Anna will tell you the entire plot of a 309-page novel called *Harry Potter and the Sorcerer's Stone*, which she has read, she confides, "seven or eight times."

And that book is only the opening chapter of a story that has become one of the most bizarre and surreal in the annals of publishing. Muggles, i.e., those who are unaware of all the wizardry afoot in the world around them, will need a brief recap if they're ever to catch up.

HISTORY OF THE HARRY POTTER BOOKS

So, in the beginning, *Harry Potter and the Sorcerer's Stone* [or *Philosopher's Stone*, as it was originally named], written by a previously unknown author named J. (for Joanne) K. Rowling, appeared in Britain in June 1997 as a juvenile-fiction title. Abracadabra! it careered to the top of the adult best-seller lists. The same eerie thing happened when the book was published September 1998 in the U.S.

Next came *Harry Potter and the Chamber of Secrets*, which proved itself, both in Britain and the U.S., as salesworthy as its predecessor. So far, the first two Harry Potter books have sold almost 2 million copies in Britain and more than 5 million in the U.S. The novels have been translated into 28 languages, including Icelandic and Serbo-Croatian. The best-seller chart in Sunday's New York *Times* Book Review [in September 1999] ranks *The Sorcerer's Stone*, in its 38th week on the list, as the No. 1–selling hardback novel and *The Chamber of Secrets*, in its 13th week, as No. 3.

But this arrangement will change almost immediately because the story keeps on developing. *Harry Potter and the Prisoner of Azkaban* (Arthur A. Levine Books/Scholastic Press; 435 pages; $19.95) finally went on sale in the U.S., exactly two months after its publication in Britain. Those U.S. readers who had not managed to obtain a copy of the British edition, chiefly through Internet orders, swamped bookstores nationwide. From El Centro, Calif., to Littleton, N.H., many stores opened for business at 12 A.M.; others offered customers tea and crumpets or steep initial discounts. Barbara Babbit Kaufman, president and founder of the Chapter 11 bookstore chain in Atlanta, reports selling more Harry Potter books in the first three hours of business than [American novelist] Tom Wolfe's novel *A Man in Full*, sold during its first day of availability last November [1998]. "Tom Wolfe's was set in Atlanta," she says, "so it was the hottest book we'd ever had." Until, that is, the new Harry Potter hit the shelves.

CONTROVERSY BEGINS

Not everyone welcomed the prospect of a third best-selling Rowling novel in the U.S. Says David Rosenthal, publisher of Simon & Schuster: "There is a big controversy stirring over whether Harry Potter should be on the New York *Times* bestseller list. There are a number of publishers—I don't happen to be among them, actually, but I've got calls about this—who are thinking about banding together to beg the New York *Times* not to include the Harry Potter books on the regular fiction best-selling list, since they now take up two slots and will soon take up a third."

The argument that a list of regular best sellers should exclude children's best sellers will strike most people as preposterous. But then the whole Harry Potter hubbub seems equally outlandish—the proliferating pages that fans are posting almost daily on the Web, the word-of-mouth testimonials from parents marveling that their nonreading children (even boys!) are tearing through the Potter books and begging for more, the confessions of a growing number of adults not so young that they find these young-adult books irresistible. And the arrival of *Harry Potter and the Prisoner of Azkaban* will only add more fuel to the Potter conflagration [a large file] and prompt anew the question that is baffling many non-Harry publishers and readers alike: What on earth is going on here?

POTTER'S POPULARITY

If there were an easy answer, nearly every other writer on earth would by now be beavering away at imitations of Rowling's formula for success, and the world would be teeming with best sellers about prepubescent wizards attending bizarre boarding schools somewhere in the north of Britain. And, in fact, it is not particularly hard to figure out the rules governing the Harry Potter books. Place appealing characters in interesting but perilous situations and leave the outcome in doubt for as long as possible. Nothing new here, nothing that storytellers as far back as [the Greek Epic poet] Homer did not grasp and gainfully employ. But, as devoted Harry Potter fans have learned, knowing a magic charm is not the same thing as performing magic. Rowling's secret is as simple and mysterious as her uncanny ability to nourish the human hunger for enchantment: she knows how to feed the desire not just to hear or read a story but to live it as well.

That is why so many people both young and naive and older and jaded have surrendered to the illusions set forth in Harry Potter's fictional world. They want to believe the unbelievable, and Rowling makes it easy and great good fun for them to do so. How pleasant to be persuaded that an orphan named Harry Potter, who has lived for 10 years with the Dursleys, his cruel aunt and uncle and their hateful son Dudley, in a faceless English suburb—specifically 4 Privet Drive, Little Whinging—learns shortly after his 11th birthday that he is really a wizard. What's more, he is famous throughout the wizard world; although his parents were murdered by the evil Lord Voldemort (so feared that he is referred to only as

"He-Who-Must-Not-Be-Named"), the infant Harry survived the attack with a lightning-bolt-shaped scar on his forehead.

Every event in the Potter books follows seamlessly from his initial self-discovery. Harry may be a skinny kid with glasses, green eyes and an unruly shock of black hair, but he also harbors uncertain potentialities. Did he thwart Voldemort's assault because of innate goodness or because he carries, even as an infant, a strain of evil more powerful than that of the Dark Wizard's? This question will remind some of the *Star Wars* films and the tangled destinies of Darth Vader and Luke Skywalker. But once such comparisons begin, they can lead in many directions.

Harry's shuttling between two worlds is also reminiscent of Lewis Carroll's Alice, L. Frank Baum's Dorothy in her journey to Oz, and the time-traveling earth children who keep reappearing in C.S. Lewis' seven-volume *The Chronicles of Narnia*. Like them, Harry is young enough both to adapt to altered realities and to observe them with a minimum of preconceptions. Also, the sorcerer's stone in the first Harry Potter book bears an obvious kinship with the all-powerful ring pursued in J.R.R. Tolkien's *Lord of the Rings* trilogy.

But Rowling's indebtedness to classical fantasy literature should not overshadow the liberties she takes with the form. Most notably, her wizard world is not at all remote from daily realities. It takes a cyclone to transport Dorothy to Oz. In contrast, Harry can walk a few steps through a London pub near Charing Cross Road and enter Diagon Alley, a wizard shopping bazaar, where he and his classmates meet late each summer to buy school supplies. And getting from there to Hogwarts is a snap; Harry and his friends go to King's Cross Station and board the *Hogwarts Express*, which departs early every September from Platform Nine and Three-Quarters.

HARRY POTTER AND THE PRISONER OF AZKABAN

It isn't necessary to have finished the first two Harry Potters before beginning *The Prisoner of Azkaban,* but it's a good idea just the same. Reading the books in proper order conveys a comforting sense of familiarity. Yep, the crenelated towers of Hogwarts look just the same as they did last year. And why not? The school is more than 1,000 years old. The academic and athletic competitions among the four Hogwarts residence houses—Gryffindor, Slytherin, Hufflepuff and Ravenclaw—remain as spirited as before. All the students are still mad about Quidditch, a hectic sport involving six goals, four moving balls and two seven-member teams careering 50 ft. or more above ground on flying broomsticks. Harry is the star player for the Gryffindor squad.

Such unchanging details make Rowling's innovations in each book seem particularly dramatic. This time out, for example, third-year students with signed permission slips from a parent or guardian are allowed periodic visits to Hogsmeade, a nearby village known as "the only entirely non-Muggle settlement in Britain." Naturally, Harry's vile Uncle Vernon refuses to sign anything relating to Hogwarts, so Harry faces the prospect of missing the fun or finding a way around the rules. And Harry meets another little problem: a dangerous killer has escaped from the wizard prison of Azkaban and is reportedly on his way to Hogwarts for the purpose of murdering Harry.

He has survived a serious threat to his life in each of the first two books, but this time Harry may be overmatched. The Azkaban prison guards, horrid hooded apparitions called dementors, have been summoned to Hogwarts to protect Harry, but he keeps fainting whenever a dementor comes near him. A sympathetic professor tells Harry why dementors merit fear: "They breed in the darkest, filthiest places, they create decay and despair, they drain peace, hope and happiness out of any human who comes too close to them. . . . Even Muggles feel their presence, though they can't see them. Get too near a dementor and every good feeling, every happy memory will be sucked out of you. You'll be left with nothing but the worst experiences of your life."

THE BOOKS AND THEIR AUTHOR

This speech is one of the darkest and most unsettling in the Potter books to date. It creates a vivid physical embodiment of a painful mental state, which Muggles call depression, and it demonstrates Rowling's considerable emotional range. She can be both genuinely scary and consistently funny, adept at both broad slapstick and allusive puns and wordplay. She appeals to the peanut gallery with such items as Bertie Bott's Every Flavor Beans, a wizard candy that means what it says on its package; it offers every flavor, ranging from chocolate and peppermint to liver and tripe and earwax. But Rowling also names the Hogwarts caretaker Argus Filch, evidently hoping that a few adult readers will remember that Argus, in Greek mythology, was a watchman with eyes all over his body. And even if no one else picks up the reference, it's the sort of touch that can prompt an author's inward smile.

"It was such fun to write," Rowling says of the first Harry Potter book. "They still are incredibly fun to write." She lives comfortably but not lavishly in Edinburgh with her daughter Jessie, 6, fending off as many outside demands on her time as she can in order to keep writing. She was completely unprepared for, and doesn't much like, all the press attention that has been mounting since she became a best-selling first novelist. During some early interviews, she mentioned that her beginning work on the Harry Potter books corresponded briefly with a bad patch in her personal life. She was newly divorced, temporarily out of work, on the dole and living in an unheated Edinburgh flat. To keep them both warm, she would wheel her young daughter into a café and sometimes jot down Harry Potter ideas on napkins.

Rowling grew annoyed when newspapers played up this anecdote as a dominant chapter in her life. "It was a great story," she concedes. "I would have liked to read it about someone else." But the tale came to define her, the product of a middle-class family and a university education, as a welfare mom who hit the jackpot. Worse, some papers began using her success as an implied criticism of poor, single women who lacked the gumption to write themselves off the dole. "That's absolute rubbish," Rowling says. "This is not vanity or arrogance, but if you look at the facts, very, very few people manage to write anything that might be a best seller. Therefore, I'm lucky by anyone's standards, let alone single mothers' standards."

Rowling says the urge to be a writer came to her early during what she describes as a "dreamy" internal childhood. She began writing stories when she was six. She also read widely, whipping through Ian Fleming [author of the James Bond novels] at age nine. Sometime later she discovered [nineteenth-century English novelist] Jane Austen, whom Rowling calls "my favorite author ever." She was writing a novel for adults when, during a 1990 train ride, "Harry Potter strolled into my head fully formed." For the next five years Rowling worked on Book One and plotted out the whole series, which will consist of seven novels, one for each year Harry spends at Hogwarts. "Those five years really went into creating a whole world. I know far more than the reader will ever need to know about ridiculous details."

Rowling insists that she never consciously set out to write for children, but that working on Harry Potter taught her how easily she could tap into her childhood memories. "I really can, with no difficulty at all, think myself back to 11 years old [Harry's age when the series opens]. You're very powerless, and kids have this whole underworld that to adults is always going to be impenetrable." That's a good description of the social setup she portrays at Hogwarts, where the students have stretches of time with little or no adult supervision. Rowling believes young people enjoy reading about peers who have a real control over their destiny. "Harry has to make his choices. He has limited access to really caring adults."

Since her characters grow a year older in each book, Rowling says that certain unavoidable changes are in store for them and the readers. A hint of what's ahead appears in *The Prisoner of Azkaban,* when Harry notices Cho Chang, the only girl on the Ravenclaw Quidditch team. "She was shorter than Harry by about a head, and Harry couldn't help noticing, nervous as he was, that she was extremely pretty. She smiled at Harry as the teams faced each other behind their captains, and he felt a slight lurch in the region of his stomach that he didn't think had anything to do with nerves."

Yes, Rowling acknowledges, Harry is on the brink of adolescence and will fall into that hormonal morass any day now. Harry and friends will notice, and do more than notice, members of the opposite sex, and the action starts in Book Four where they all fall in love with the wrong people. A foolishly smitten or moony Harry may challenge the devotion of the readers who admire his innocent, boyish virtues and unflappable dignity, except, perhaps, those readers who have grown into adolescents themselves.

But Harry Potter fans have something a good deal more worrisome to fret about than potential smooching and hand holding. Rowling has been dropping increasingly pointed promises that the four remaining Harry Potter books will turn darker than the first three. "There will be deaths," she says. "I am writing about someone, Voldemort, who is evil. And rather than make him a pantomime villain, the only way to show how evil it is to take a life is to kill someone the reader cares about." Can she possibly mean (oh!) Hermione, (no!) Ron or (gasp!) Harry himself? Rowling discloses nothing, but she does note that the children who contact her "are always most worried I'm going to kill Ron. It shows how sharp they are. They've watched so many movies where the hero's best friend gets killed."

HARRY POTTER ON FILM

And certain Potter purists are concerned about Harry's upcoming first appearance on the silver screen. British producer David Heyman saw a blurb on *The Sorcerer's Stone* shortly after its British publication but before the book became a smash. He brought the project to Warner Bros. (like *Time*, owned by Time Warner), which optioned the book. The plan is for a live-action film, with Harry played as a British schoolboy. A first script, by Steven Kloves, who wrote and directed *The Fabulous Baker Boys*, is due by the end of the year [1999].

Heyman says Warner Bros. "has already got a lot of calls from parents wanting their kids to be in the movie." But, he says, "the good news is it's not a star-driven film. It's the child's film, and the child is not going to command a $20 million fee. So the primary cost will be in the special effects. We want to make all of that as believable and fantastical as possible. Technology is now incredible."

But one of the interesting things about Hogwarts in the Potter books is that it contains no technology at all. Light is provided by torches and heat by massive fireplaces. Who needs electricity when you have plenty of wizards and magic wands? Who, for that matter, requires mail pickup and delivery when a squadron of trained owls flies messages to and from the school? Technology is for Muggles, who rely on contraptions because they cannot imagine the conveniences of magic. Who wouldn't choose a wizard's life?

The *Harry Potter* Books and the Series Tradition

Jim Trelease

In this excerpt from the fifth edition of his highly success-ful how-to for adults who wish to read to children, *The Read-Aloud Handbook*, Jim Trelease places *Harry Potter* within the long tradition of series books. Trelease distin-guishes between two types of series books: those churned out in quantity, often by more than one author under a single pen name, and others, more sophisticated, written by one author "and characterized by richer text, plot, and characterization." *Harry Potter*, Trelease determines, be-longs to the latter category. Trelease notes that series books of either category have always come under fire from cer-tain adults who believe that reading them, and not the so-called classics, will corrupt the minds of young adults. But among the many lessons Trelease draws from the *Harry Potter* books is that many adults devoured series books when they were young and have fared no worse for this supposed waste of time. In fact, he argues, these books of-ten provide an important and accessible gateway for chil-dren to enter into the fascinating world of book reading again and again. Jim Trelease's *Read-Aloud Handbook* has been a valuable guide to parents since its release in 1979. Trelease works full-time addressing parents, teachers, and professional groups on the subjects of children, literature, and television.

Every decade seems to produce reading material that pro-vokes the wrath of parents, teachers, and librarians, all of whom are absolutely certain these books will corrupt children's reading and souls to the core. Back in the 1940s and 1950s it was comic books. In the 1980s it was The Baby-Sitters Club and Sweet Valley High books, in the 1990s the Goosebumps, and now it's Harry Potter in 2000.

How Is Harry Potter Different from Other "Series" Books?

There are two kinds of series books:

1. The quick-and-easy commercial kind like Nancy Drew, Goosebumps, and The Baby-Sitters Club.
2. The more sophisticated series like [Beverly] Cleary's Ramona books, [C.S.] Lewis's The Chronicles of Narnia, [Lynn Reid] Banks's *The Indian in the Cupboard*, and Rowling's Harry Potter.

The quick-and-easy series are often mass-produced, sometimes written by more than one author, and churned out at a pace of more than one a year; the books in a more sophisticated series are always written by one person, published a year or more apart, and characterized by richer text, plot, and characterization.

Along with its excellent imagery, what especially sets Harry Potter books apart from nearly all other series books is the amount of text. Consuming that many words, students are getting prodigiously better at reading—many for the first time—and *enjoying* it.

Some critics have complained that J.K. Rowling's language is not classical. True, her sentences are largely unadorned and, except for proper nouns, there is less for the reader to *stumble over*. And that's good. Stumbling over text is a discouragement for young readers, not an incentive. And while classics like [Swiss author Johanna Spyri's] *Heidi* have heavier, more adorned text, when was the last time you saw a kid reading *Heidi* in the airport? I saw five kids reading the fourth Harry Potter book in airports on July 10, 2000. A classic that is unread is like an unheard concert. In order for medicine to do any good, it must be absorbed. To get a lot better at reading, children must read a lot of words.

Before someone exclaims, "I've read *Heidi* and Harry's no *Heidi*," I'm not talking about the book's literary style or imagery, not even its emotional levels—just the number of words a child must traverse in order to reach the end. Here's a word count I did on some books, including a few classics:

> *Goosebumps:* 8 words per sentence; 22,450 words in book.
>
> *Heidi:* 19.6 words per sentence; 93,600 words in book.
>
> *The Hobbit:* 18 words per sentence; 97,470 words in book.
>
> *The Hunchback of Notre Dame:* 15 words per sentence; 126,000 words in book.
>
> *Harry Potter and the Goblet of Fire:* 13 words per sentence; 181,000 words in book.

Lesson No. 1: *Harry Potter has children willingly reading books that are eight times longer than* Goosebumps *and twice as long as* Heidi.

Is Harry Potter a Classic?

"Classic" has about as many definitions as there are tastes. Classics have been variously described as: the wisest of counselors; the telescopes and charts by which we navigate the dangerous seas of life; the keys to the palace of wisdom; and the means by which we elevate the mind.

I'm not sure Harry fits any of those definitions, though he certainly keeps children's minds and vocabularies from sinking. But there's a definition of a classic I like best of all, perhaps because it's more democratic. It comes from Columbia's legendary professor of English, Mark Van Doren: "A classic is a book that stays in print."

That is, if it continually meets people's needs, generation after generation, regardless of whether the critics liked it or not, and they keep buying it, publishers keep it in print. Only time and sales will tell if Harry is a classic—or they issue a *Cliffs Notes* for it.

In the debate over whether Harry Potter is a classic, one thing that has been ignored is Harry's competition. I have to wonder how many classics could have survived what Harry faced at the turn of the millennium:

- 98 percent of homes have a television, most offering thirty cable channels or more.
- 50 percent of children's bedrooms have a TV.
- Annual video sales outnumber book sales.
- More and more teens have cellular phones and pagers.
- Internet use is doubling every one hundred days.
- Shopping malls are open seven days and six nights a week.

Lesson No. 2: *Children will choose a book over TV if the book is interesting enough.*

WHY ARE THE POTTER BOOKS SO POPULAR?

The fantasy is rich and the cheeky humor (with a dollop of [English author] Roald Dahl thrown in) is very appealing, but there's something else, too. Shortly after Harry's initial success, and while many adults were pondering his fortune (the *Horn Book*, the distinguished children's literature journal, wouldn't give Harry a starred review), a Texas library professor made a simple but insightful observation: The Harry Potter books are entirely "plot-driven."

This isn't to say such a condition is good or bad, but it may account for many children's reactions to the series. When we adults want to enjoy ourselves with print, relax on the beach, or in front of a roaring fire on a winter afternoon, many of us choose a novel that will have us turning pages, forgetting what time it is, and reading into the wee hours. In such circumstances we don't want issue-driven novels or complex studies of human character. We want a good, plot-driven book when we read for pleasure.

But what do the adults foist on students? Issue- or character-driven novels, awarded prizes for their complexity and character study. This is not to say such volumes are either bad or ill-chosen, but where in the name of Uncle Newbery are the plot-driven books on the award lists? (I might point out, the most popular Newbery winners are the ones with strong plot lines.) It's okay for adults to read such books, but children should be reading for learning, enrichment, and insight—not for the pure pleasure of turning pages to find out what happens next. As Harry might say, "Oh, those stupid muggles!"

Lesson No. 3: *Children want page-turners, just like grown-ups do.*

There is a difference between "can" and "should," and the latter is what's more appropriate. When the Potter books first arrived in the U.S., talk-show host Rosie O'Donnell declared her everlasting love for Harry (terrific, I thought) and announced she'd just finished reading it to her four-year-old son (I shuddered).

Many of the concepts in the Potter books—class rivalries, sibling rivalries, child abuse, orphanhood, and generational inheritance—are beyond the grasp of very young children. Why not wait until the child is old enough to bring a frame of reference and maturity to the book so it can be fully enjoyed instead of just wondered at?

Furthermore, the realistic fantasy in the books can be frightening to any child too young to make the distinction between fantasy and reality. The author herself didn't feel it appropriate to read Harry to her daughter until she was almost seven years old.

Lesson No. 4: *Unlike Beanie Babies, Harry Potter books are not for all ages.*

ARE THE POTTER BOOKS REALLY A THREAT TO CHILDREN'S SOULS?

The writer Anna Quindlen once wisely noted, "There is nothing so wonderful in America that someone can't create a

Calvary out of it." So when thirty-five million children lay down their Walkmans, cell phones, remotes, and Gameboys to read 400-page books (Harry Potters), the doomsayers shout, "It's the Devil wearing the Messiah's clothes!"

Anything new, popular, or magical becomes the anti-Christ—which is not peculiar to our time or place. The furor over the Potter books reminded me of a similar one in 1847, when Sir James Young Simpson introduced pain-killing anesthetics to the maternity ward. He was immediately accused by church leaders of circumventing God's will (If God imposes pain in childbirth, who is man to nullify it?). Today, Simpson's innovative practices are commonly used in both Christian and secular hospitals throughout the world.

The issue of censorship and children's books is greater than we have space for here (see my essay at www.trelease-on-reading.com/censor1.html), so for now, suffice it to say: Since the arrival of the Potter books, violent crime is at a record thirty-year low, there's been no increase in juvenile crime, and none of the boys who murdered their classmates and teachers in recent years were reading the Potter books. Additionally, the thousands of midnight Potter-parties in bookstores on July 8, 2000, were marked by nothing but orderly, good-humored behavior on the part of the children and their parents—something that probably couldn't have been said about a similar gathering of 100,000 children and parents at a thousand midnight Little League games.

WHAT'S WRONG WITH SERIES BOOKS IN THE FIRST PLACE?

That question is best answered by the award-winning research of Dr. Catherine Sheldrick Ross, acting dean of graduate studies and professor of library and information science, at the University of Western Ontario, Canada.

Ross found "series books" to be the uncontested favorite of young readers for the last one hundred years, but acknowledges they have long been the object of scorn by the cultural gatekeepers—teachers and librarians. That long-term antagonism is worth exploring if you wish to understand children's reading patterns.

According to Ross, around the time of the Civil War and coinciding with significant revolutions in printing and delivery services (like the railroads), there appeared a new kind of reading material: cheap fiction called the "story papers" and "dime novels." Printed on inexpensive pulp paper, these stories of adventure-bound heroes and heroines appealed to the servant and labor classes—the very people ignored by traditional publishers. Immediately these newfound appetites for reading were scorned by the upper classes and attacked as dangerous.

The papers, fictional forerunners of today's daily and supermarket tabloids, contained serialized adventure tales. With their "blood and thunder" tales of cowboys and Indians, pirates, outlaws, and triumphant orphans, the papers and dime novels were published bi-weekly, became national sensations, and annually sold into the millions. Instead of rejoicing at the idea of millions of unlettered citizens beginning the reading habit, social critics denounced the trend and predicted disaster.

The offspring of the dime novel was the "series book" for young readers, conceived by Edward Stratemeyer in the late 1890s. Aimed at the preteen and teen reader, the series books eventually included Nancy Drew, The Hardy Boys, The Bobbsey Twins, The Motor Boys, The Rover Boys, Tom Swift, and the Outdoor Girls. The stories were adventure- or family-oriented, written nonstop by a large syndicate of writers, all using pseudonyms.

Just as social critics condemned dime novels, librarians and teachers denounced the series books. Franklin K. Mathiews, chief librarian of the Boy Scouts of America, wrote in 1914: "I wish I could label each one of these books: 'Explosive! Guaranteed to Blow Your Boy's Brains Out.' . . . [A]s some boys read such books, their imaginations are literally 'blown out' and they go into life as terribly crippled as though by some material explosion they had lost a hand or foot."

Fifteen years later, the elitists were so certain Nancy Drew would corrupt girls' minds (as sixty years later they would think Goosebumps would turn every child into a serial killer), H.W. Wilson Company, the largest U.S. manufacturer of library supplies, refused to print the index cards for the card catalog for Nancy Drew, and even published a list of nearly sixty authors who should not be circulated by libraries, all of them authors of series like Tom Swift and the Bobbsey Twins.

Coupled with the elitism was the widely held belief that fiction was something to be fed to children in only small, controlled doses. They believed children only learned from *facts;* therefore, fiction was useless. And the worst fiction of all would be the sensational fiction of series books. Here's a quote from 1850: "No part of education . . . is of greater importance than the selection of proper books. . . . No dissipation can be worse than that induced by the perusal of exciting books of fiction . . . a species of a monstrous and erroneous nature."

What made the series books especially evil for children was that they were "addictive." Children weren't content to read just one; they'd read the first, then the second, then the third, and so on. Unfortunately, moaned the experts, the whole time they're reading that junk, they're *not* reading the wonderful nonfiction book on sponges that just arrived in the library!

Lesson No. 5: *The fear that Harry and series books will corrupt the soul is at least as old as the Bobbsey Twins.*

WHY DON'T KIDS READ THE CLASSICS ANYMORE?

If you think America's children were huddled in corners with their classics until television arrived in the 1950s, you're wrong. They were reading, but not the classics. Way back, they were reading those infamous "Frank Merriwell" dime novels cranked out weekly by William Gilbert Patten under the pen name of Burt L. Standish. For all her imagination, J.K. Rowling still has a way to go to equal the stamina of Patten: He wrote 776 of the titles, and sales often reached as high as 125,000 copies a week.

How much damage these mindless adventure stories might do was hotly debated, but not by young Jacques, who was fresh off the boat from France and soaking up every Merriwell novel he could find. Nor was he ashamed years later to admit the profoundly positive influence the books played in his reading development and acclimation to America, except by then he was well on his way to becoming America's best known humanities scholar—Jacques Barzun (who turned ninety-six in 2000 and celebrated by producing a bestseller on the history of world culture).

If you think today's best writers were all reading the classics as children, guess again. A few years ago at an event at the Museum of the City of New York, two men were huddled together talking. There were perhaps no two people in the room more disparate than they.

One was Louis Auchincloss, son of a corporate lawyer and one himself, a Yale graduate, novelist, biographer, essayist, and president of the Museum of the City of New York. He's been described as the closest thing this age can offer in the way of Henry James, Edith Wharton, and Anthony Trollope.

His partner in conversation was Pete Hamill, eighteen years his junior, son of impoverished Irish immigrants, college dropout, a sheet-metal worker, advertising designer, journalist, and New York newspaper editor. While Auchincloss spent much of his life writing about boardrooms and bankers, Hamill won awards for writing about the Bowery and boozers. Yet here they were, deep in conversation. About what? If you'd been close enough to eavesdrop, you'd have heard them discussing the fact that Auchincloss had just found a used copy of *Bomba the Jungle Boy at the Death Swamp*, the favorite series from both of their childhoods.

On the other hand, if you think the adults were all home reading books when TV arrived, a Gallup poll in 1952 reported only 18 percent of the adults were presently reading a novel when surveyed, and in 1963 less than half the adults had finished a book in the last year. By contrast, in 1999 that figure had climbed to 84 percent.

Lesson No. 6: *They really weren't reading all that much in the good old days (but they sure are now, thanks to Harry, Oprah, and user-friendly bookstores).*

DO SERIES BOOKS ACTUALLY DO ANY GOOD OR JUST TAKE UP KIDS' TIME?

Certainly series books make a "pleasure" connection with the child. . . . Humans seldom do something over and over unless it brings repeated pleasures. Pleasure is the "glue" that holds us to a particular activity. . . .

A study of eleven- and twelve-year-olds' reading habits showed they chose series books because they were easier to find and they already knew something about the book (its characters and setting). With this advance knowledge, they had a head start on the reading. Ross's research shows that young readers frequently complain about the difficulty in starting a new book, getting through the early chapters and meeting the characters. In a familiar series, this difficulty is averted. This "instant start" instead of frustration plays a large role in luring some students into regular reading.

And finally, Ross points to the large chunks of reading done by the series reader as examples of what Margaret Meek called "private lessons." That is, these daily readings teach the child the rules about skimming and inferring, about where one must slow down to decipher the clues, about the importance of chapter titles or of character and setting. The adage that "the more you read, the better you get at it" is not only true, but it should be the slogan of series books.

It's amazing that the critics of series books have never caught on to the simple biblical message that forbidden fruit is often that much more appealing. But they also don't understand that some of the very best readers are produced by such books, and eventually graduate on to better books. In

1926, the American Library Association asked 36,750 students from thirty-four cities to name their favorite books. Ninety-eight percent listed one of the mass-produced Stratemeyer series books (The Rover Boys; The Motor Boys; Tom Swift; and the Bobbsey Twins), with the high-IQ students reading twice as many of the series books.

Updating that to the present, as part of its annual "Read Across America" promotion, the National Education Association asked student participants to name their favorite books. From the 8,100 titles they nominated, the NEA culled the top 100, which ran from No. 1 (Harry Potter) to No. 100 (*Sarah Plain and Tall* by Patricia MacLachlin). Among the top 100 titles, 35 percent were series books, including Potter, Goosebumps, Arthur, the Berenstain Bears, and American Girls. It's worth noting that the books were nominated by the readers, not the "I-hate-reading" kids.

Over a five-year period, I surveyed 2,887 teachers, with an average of fourteen years' teaching experience. When asked to name the favorite books from their own childhoods, 30 percent named a series book as their personal childhood favorite. Since a recent study shows teachers' literacy skills to be the equal of their college classmates, and 50 percent of the teachers' skills exceed 80 percent of the general population's, it should be obvious that series books do not impede literacy.

The most conclusive evidence of series books' ability to produce *better* readers can be found in the thirty years of research done by Professor G. Robert Carlson. Each semester he asked his graduate students to write their "reading autobiographies," recollections of their early years with reading—what they loved and what they hated. As he reports in *Voices of Readers: How We Come to Love Books*, the majority of these students had strong relationships with series books in their early years. Did it stunt their intellectual growth? Well, if they made it all the way to graduate school, apparently not.

Lesson No. 7: *Series books are avidly read by the best readers, without impeding their skills.*

So I Should Read Series Books to My Class?

That depends on which kind you're going to read. The cheap commercial ones are best left to the children to find on their own—and they will. No one needed to read Goosebumps to their classes. Kids walk into second grade already knowing about them. There is a built-in magnet between kids and junk; they can find each other in the dark—junk food, junk clothes, junk music, junk hairstyles.

The real job of the parent and teacher is to get the child ready for the magic moment. And the magic moment occurs when, after reading the thirty-fifth book in a series, the child turns to a best friend and confides, "Do you ever get the feeling it's like reading the same book, over and over?" At that point, they're ready to move up. But if they don't know there is an "up" to move to, they're stuck in a rut. So while they're reading Goosebumps or Baby-Sitters to themselves, you're reading aloud to them from better literature.

I do think the *quality* series, like Harry Potter or Indian in the Cupboard—and the Magic Treehouse for kindergartners—are fine for reading aloud. Reading aloud the first book in such a series is a very good way of whetting their appetites to go and read the rest of the series on their own if they are capable of doing that.

Lesson No. 8: *When reading aloud, avoid the "junk" series; the kids will find those on their own.*

The Fascinating Language of *Harry Potter*

Jessy Randall

In this article, Jessy Randall explores the meaning and origins of J.K. Rowling's quirky vocabulary of the wizard world. Beginning with the word *Muggle*, which has already entered into English usage and is a solid candidate for inclusion in standard dictionaries, Randall explores Rowling's choice of words. The words and names Rowling uses come from several languages and her language contains allusions to mythology and poetry. Names, in particular, are often excellent clues as to what the reader should expect from Rowling's characters. Rowling's invented language constitutes passwords for Muggles to enter into and fully participate in the wizard world of Harry Potter. Jessy Randall has worked as a rare book librarian at Colorado College and has published numerous poems in addition to articles about language.

The *Harry Potter* books, so mind-bogglingly popular in England, the United States, and all over the world, are not just good literature but a treasury of wordplay and invention. In naming her characters, beasts, spells, places, and objects, author J.K. Rowling makes use of Latin, French, and German words, poetic devices, and language jokes. It is not necessary to pick up on the wordplay to enjoy the series—indeed, it is unlikely that most young people, or adults for that matter, have noticed everything there is to notice. Rowling herself may not be sure of the origins of some of the vocabulary. She said in an amazon.com interview, "It is always hard to tell

Jessy Randall, "Wizard Words: The Literary, Latin, and Lexical Origins of Harry Potter's Vocabulary," *Verbatim*, vol. 26, Spring 2001, pp. 1–7. Copyright © 2001 by Verbatim Magazine. Reproduced by permission.

what your influences are. Everything you've seen, experienced, read, or heard gets broken down like compost in your head and then your own ideas grow out of that compost."

MUGGLE: AN OLD WORD, A NEW WORD

Even those who have not read a word of *Harry Potter* may, at this point, be familiar with the term *Muggle*, which is used to describe nonmagic people, places, and things. Literary agent Jane Lebowitz is quoted in *We Love Harry Potter* saying that *Muggle* has already become part of her family's everyday vocabulary. This word is the most likely candidate from the series to become a permanent part of the English language, and is currently in consideration for inclusion in a future edition of the *Merriam-Webster's Collegiate Dictionary.*

We first hear the word *Muggle* in the first book in the series, *Harry Potter and the Sorcerer's Stone*. In chapter four, the friendly giant, Hagrid, shows up at Harry's home to take him to wizard school, warning Harry's Uncle Vernon not to get in the way:

"I'd like ter see a great Muggle like you stop him," he said.

"A what?" said Harry, interested.

"A Muggle," said Hagrid, "it's what we call nonmagic folks like them. An' it's your bad luck you grew up in a family o' the biggest Muggles I ever laid eyes on."

So *Muggle* is not just a descriptive term, it's a pejorative— an insult. And, as with stupidity or coarseness, there are degrees of Mugglehood.

(Naturally, a person can't help being born Muggle or wizard, and in the fourth book in the series, *Harry Potter and the Goblet of Fire*, the wizard community debates whether all Muggles are inherently bad. The darker wizard forces believe the wizard "race" to be superior, and want to wipe out all Muggles. Their logic is, of course, flawed, since Muggle parents can have wizard children—Harry's friend Hermione Granger is one such *mudblood*. The reverse is also true: Argus Filch, caretaker at Hogwarts, tries to hide the fact that he is a *squib*, a wizard-born child who lacks wizard powers. A damp squib in English slang is a firework that fails to explode when lit, or a joke that fails to come off, or any enterprise that fails. Argus, by the way, is a hundred-eyed giant in Greek mythology, and *filch*, of course, is a slang term for the act of petty thieving.)

But back to *Muggle*. It turns out that Rowling did not invent the word, although she may not have been aware of its early meanings. It was the Kentish [a dialect of English spoken in the region of Kent] word for tail in the 13th century (also appearing as *moggle*) and, believe it or not, was English and American slang for marijuana as early as 1926 and as late as 1972. Mystery writers Raymond Chandler and Ed McBain used the word this way ("the desk clerk's a muggle-smoker"; "Some kid was shoving muggles . . ."), and perhaps Louis Armstrong's 1928 record "Muggles" made use of this meaning. A *mugglehead* was someone who smoked pot; a *muggler* was an addict.

Why does the word work so well to describe unwizardly culture? Perhaps because it echoes so many low, earthly words. In the 19th century, a *muggins* was a fool or simpleton. *Mugwort* and *mugweed* are names for the common plant also known as wormwood. *Muggle* sounds like a combination of *mud, muddle, mug* (a slang term for face or especially grimace; photographs of criminals are *mug-shots*), *bug* (the Buggles recorded "Video Killed the Radio Star" in 1979—but that seems beside the point), *Mugsy* (a common gangster nickname in film and television—also a character from Bugs Bunny cartoons, whose repeated line is "Duh, okay boss"), and *Mudville* (where Casey struck out). It's difficult, in fact, to find an echo of anything airy or light in the word, so it's a good one to describe regular, boring, nonmagic aspects of life.

CHARACTERS

Many of the less important characters in the series have alliterative, almost tongue-twister names. These include Harry's nasty, gluttonous cousin Dudley Dursley; his fellow Hogwarts students Colin Creevey, Gladys Gudgeon, Cho Chang, and the twins, Parvati and Padma Patil; Poppy Pomfrey, the school nurse; Florean Fortescue, who owns the ice cream parlor; Peter Pettigrew, the rat *animagus* (a wizard who can turn into an animal at will—combination of *animal* and *mage* or *magus*, magician); and Bathilda Bagshot, author of the wizard textbook, *A History of Magic*. In the fourth book in the series, the rhyme goes internal: Rita Skeeter is the troublesome journalist who puts Harry in no small danger. "Miss Skeeter" echoes *mosquito*, a similarly bloodthirsty pest, and indeed, Skeeter is an animagus who takes the form of an insect. More wordplay: she uses this ability in order to *bug*—listen in on— conversations at the wizard school.

The four founders of Hogwarts also have alliterative names: Godric Gryffindor, Helga Hufflepuff, Rowena Ravenclaw, and Salazar Slytherin. It is for these characters that the four houses of the school are named: Gryffindor (for the brave—this is where Harry, Ron, and Hermione are placed), Hufflepuff (for the loyal), Slytherin (for the ambitious), and Ravenclaw (for the witty). A *griffin* or *gryphon*, by the way, is half lion, half eagle, and according to legend is the sworn enemy of the (sly and slithering) snake. And speaking of snakes, a snake named Nagina attacks Harry—this name echoes that of Nag, the cobra in Rudyard Kipling's short story "Rikki-Tikki-Tavi."

Harry and those close to him have less cartoonish names. Their names do not give them away. The Potters—Harry and his parents, James and Lily—share a surname with a neighbor family of Rowling's girlhood. Harry's friends Ron Weasley and Hermione Granger have non-coded names: Ron is extremely loyal, exhibiting no weasel-like qualities; Hermione has little in common with the daughter of Helen of Troy, nor with the Shakespeare character of the same name.

Many of the professors at Hogwarts, on the other hand, have particularly telling names. Severus Snape (*severe, snipe, snub*) is an unpleasant and strict teacher who keeps getting passed over for promotion. Vindictus Veridian (*vindictive*, green with jealousy) teaches a class on curses and counter-curses. Professor Sprout runs Herbology. Professor Quirrel is quarrelsome and squirrely. Alastor Moody (*alastor* is Greek for avenging deity) waits many years for his chance to take revenge. Gilderoy Lockhart, the Defense Against the Dark Arts teacher in the second book, *Harry Potter and the Chamber of Secrets*, is vanity incarnate. Indeed, his name sounds like that of a character in a Harlequin romance. The Gild in Gilderoy echoes *gilding the lily*, gratuitous excess—and also *gilt*, fake gold. Certainly Gilderoy is far from worthy of the love and adoration he feels for himself.

Harry's nemesis at school is Draco Malfoy, a name that screams evil: the first part sounds like *dragon* (and indeed, *draco* is Latin for dragon, and Draconian Law, named after the Athenian lawyer Draco, is known for its harshness), the second, like *malevolent, malignant*, or *malfeasance*. Also, *mal foi* is French for 'bad faith.' Draco's toadies are Crabbe and Goyle, echoes of *crab* (as in crabby, grumpy) and *gargoyle*. His father's name is Lucius, which echoes *Lucifer*, a name for the devil; his mother's name is Narcissa, as in *narcissistic*. (By the way: the Malfoys' elf-slave in the second book in the series, *Harry Potter and the Chamber of Secrets*, is named Dobby, an alternate term for *brownie*, or house elf, in certain parts of England.)

The most evil character of all, Voldemort, is usually identified simply as *he-who-must-not-be-named* or *you-know-who*—clearly, for many people, names have a certain power of their own. (Harry himself never subscribes to this belief.) Voldemort actually has several names; at one point he is known as Tom Marvolo Riddle, an anagram for "I am Lord Voldemort." Each piece of Voldemort's name, broken down, sounds rather unappealing: a *vole* is a rodent, and *mort* is Latin for death. If we treat the name as a loose anagram, we can also pull out *mole, mold*, and *vile*. *Vol de mort* is French for 'flight from death,' and indeed, Voldemort manages to escape death repeatedly.

So, names can give away the good or evil nature of a character—and, because nothing in the *Harry Potter* series is that simple, they can also fool you. Language scholars will not be too surprised to learn that Remus Lupin turns out to be a werewolf. According to legend, Romulus and Remus—the founders of Rome—were suckled by a wolf, and the Latin word for wolf is *lupus*. But those who know their plant life may associate him with the *lupin*, a pretty lilac-like flower, and indeed, the Professor, despite his tendency to turn beastly at the full moon, is a good, harmless soul.

Similarly, Sirius Black (*serious, black*) has a name that makes him sound like a terrible villain and is assumed to be so for most of the third book in the series, *Harry Potter and the Prisoner of Azkaban*. He turns out, however, to be quite the opposite. Black is an animagus who can take the form of a dog (which explains his nickname of Padfoot), and Sirius (Latin, 'burning') is the formal name for the dog star, the brightest star in the constellation Canis Major ('big dog').

Albus Dumbledore is another tricky one. Despite his name, he is most certainly not dumb. He is the "Supreme Mugwump, International Confed. of Wizards" and the head of Hogwarts. *Albus* is Latin for white; *dumbledore* is an old English word for bumblebee.

Some of the animal names in the series allude to literary or historical characters. The cat who wanders the halls of Hogwarts is Mrs. Norris, very probably named after a character from Jane Austen, Rowling's favorite author. Like the cat, Fanny Price's Aunt Norris in *Mansfield Park* is a terrible busybody of unparalleled nosiness. Hermione's cat is Crookshanks, probably named after the 19th-century English caricaturist George Cruikshank, best known for his illustrations of fairy tales and [English novelist] Charles Dickens's *Oliver Twist*. (In the "Splendid Strolling" chapter of John Forster's *The Life of Charles Dickens*, Mr. Wilson tells Mrs. Gamp that it was "The great George . . . the Crookshanks" who escorted her into her carriage.) *Crookshanks* is also an old-fashioned insult meaning 'crooked shanks' or 'crooked legs.' In the translations of the *Harry Potter* books, Hermione's cat is named variations on this insult: *Krummbein* in German, *Knikkebeen* in Dutch, *Skeivskank* in Norwegian, and *Koukkujalka* in Finnish.

Spells

Most of the spells in the *Harry Potter* books are based on English or Latin, and so the meanings are fairly straightforward. *Reducio!* (Latin *reducere*) reduces the size of an object, for example. *Engorgio!* (Old French *engorgier*) engorges or enlarges it. *Reparo!* (Latin *reparare*) repairs. *Riddikulus!* (Latin *ridiculus*) turns an enemy—usually a Boggart—into something ridiculous or laughable. *Lumos!* (Latin *lumen*, 'light') causes illumination. *Impedimenta!* (Latin *impedimentum*) impedes or slows the enemy. *Sonorus!* (Latin *sonor*, 'sound;' English *sonorous*) causes one's wand to become a microphone. *Stupefy!* (Latin *stupefacere, stupere*, 'to be stunned') stupefies the enemy, causing confusion. *Expelliarmus!* (Latin *expellere*, 'to drive out') expels your opponent's wand from his or her hand.

And then there are the three spells that wizards are forbidden to use on each other: *Imperio!* (Latin *imperium*, 'command;' English *imperious*) gives total power. *Crucio!* (Latin *cruciere*, 'to crucify or torture,' from *crux*, 'cross;' English *excruciating*) causes pain; and *Avada Kedavra* is the death spell. This last term in Aramaic means 'Let the thing be destroyed;' it weirdly echoes the magic word every school child knows, *abracadabra*, but incorporates the sound of *cadaver*. (*Abracadabra* is an extremely old word of unknown origin. It may derive from the Aramaic; it may just be a nonsense sound. Another possibility is that the repeated *abras* stand for the first sounds of the Hebrew letters signifying Father, Son, and Holy Ghost: *Ab, Ben, Ruach*, and *Acadosch*. The first documented appearance of *abracadabra* is in a 2nd-century poem by Q. Severus Samonicus. It is still in use as a magical word today.) A fourth evil spell is *Morsmordre!* which sends the "dark mark"—a skull with a snake coming out of its mouth—into the sky. It is a combination of *mors,* Latin 'death,' and *mordre,* French 'to bite.' The word also echoes Mordred, the name of King Arthur's illegitimate son and enemy, and Mordor, the evil area of [English writer J.R.R.] Tolkien's Middle Earth, "where the shadows lie." Mordred and Mordor, in turn, echo *murder.*

There are, of course, a great many more spells beyond these, some used only once or twice in the entire series. *Furnunculus!* for example, causes horrible boils to erupt all over a victim's skin, and a *furunculus* (lacking the first *n* in the spell word) is a type of boil. *Tarantallegra!* (*tarantula,* 'spider;' *tarantella,* Spanish dance; *allegro,* musical term for 'fast,' from the Italian) causes the victim's legs to dance uncontrollably. *Waddiwasi!* in one case sends a wad of gum out of a keyhole and up a particular victim's nose. *Peskipiksi Pesternomi!* ("pesky pixies, pester not me") is useful for handling Cornish pixies.

PLACES

Rowling has some of her greatest fun in naming places. The despicable Dursleys, Harry's adoptive family, live in Little Whinging, Surrey (*whingeing* is British English for *whining*). Dudley Dursley (who is certainly a dud) proudly attends Smeltings School, which is a clever play on the idea of the finishing school, since to *smelt* is to refine, as in ore. *Smelt* as a noun is a type of fish, and as a verb is the British English past tense of *smell.* So Smeltings is a stinky finishing school, perfect for Dudley's alma mater.

To meet his wizarding needs, Harry visits the shops in Diagon Alley (*diagonally*) and Knockturn Alley (*nocturnally*) before setting up residence at Hogwarts, the wizard school. Hogwarts, an inversion of *warthogs*, also contains the ideas of *hog* and *warts*—in fact, the first line of the school song is "Hogwarts, Hogwarts, Hoggy Warty Hogwarts."

Other wizard schools are Beauxbatons (French for 'beautiful wands') and Durmstrang (an inversion of the German *Sturm und Drang,* 'storm and stress,' also the name of a German literary movement in the 18th century whose followers included Goethe and Schiller).

The name of *Azkaban,* the wizard jail, echoes that of Alcatraz, the supposedly inescapable American prison off the coast of San Francisco. Azkaban is guarded by Dementors (who can make you demented).

To travel from place to place, wizards may use Floo Powder, which transports them magically from one chimney flue to another. Perhaps Rowling was thinking of the old tongue-twister limerick, which goes, in one version:

> A flea and a fly in a flue
> Were caught, so what could they do?
> Said the flea, "let us fly!"
> Said the fly, "let us flee!"
> So they flew through a flaw in the flue.

OTHER STUFF

Wizard candies have the same kind of exuberant, lyrical names as those in [British writer] Roald Dahl's books. *Fizzing whizbies* are sherbet balls that make you levitate—strong echoes of the Fizzy Lifting Drink in *Charlie and the Chocolate Factory.* Everlasting Gobstoppers may not be available, but Hogwarts students do enjoy *Bertie Bott's Every Flavor Beans* (in flavors including marmalade, spinach, liver, tripe, sprouts, toast, curry, grass, sardine, and earwax), *Drooble's Best Blowing Gum, Chocolate Frogs, Pumpkin Pasties, Cauldron Cakes, Toothflossing Stringmints,* and *Pepper Imps.* Harry and his friends also drink frothy mugs of *butterbeer,* a play on *butterscotch* and *root beer.*

In sports, the Hogwarts students have *Quidditch*—a wizard form of soccer—involving *Bludgers* (who bludgeon), *Beaters* (who beat) and the *Golden Snitch,* which Harry, as *Seeker,* has to snatch out of the sky. To do this, he rides his

Nimbus 2000 broomstick, *nimbus* meaning 'radiant light,' or a type of cloud.

Besides broomsticks, magical objects found around Hogwarts include the *Mirror of Erised*, which shows what you most desire. *Erised*, of course, is *desire* backward. Harry sees his parents in the mirror and briefly believes them to be alive, until he figures out the secret of the mirror. Hermione, Ron, and Harry make use of a *Polyjuice* potion, which changes them into other shapes; *poly* means many, as in *polyglot* (many languages) or *polygamy* (many spouses). The *Remembrall* is a crystal-ball-like device that turns red when one has forgotten to do something; it is a ball that helps you remember all. And *Spellotape*—a sticky substance used to mend wands and so on—is a play on *Sellotape*, a British brand of cellulose (American *Scotch*) tape. Other magical objects include *Mrs. Skower's* [scours] *All-Purpose Magical Mess Remover*, the *Pocket Sneakoscope*, the *Put-Outer*, and the *Revealer* (the opposite of an eraser).

PASSWORDS

Along with learning spells and the names of magical objects, wizards-in-training have to memorize passwords. To get into the common room of Gryffindor House at Hogwarts, Harry must pass the Fat Lady, a talking portrait of a woman in a pink dress who usually makes up the passwords. Her choices include the fairly simple *banana fritters, pig snout,* and *wattlebird* along with the more evocative *balderdash* and *flibbertigibbet*. *Balderdash* in the 16th century was a jumbled mixture of liquors, but by the 17th century it had come to mean a jumbled mixture of words, and by the 19th it meant obscene language. *Flibbertigibbet*, too, was a 16th century representation of meaningless chatter; it also meant a chattering person, more specifically a prattling woman, or—now quite obsolete—it could be the name of a devil or demon (in Act III, scene iv, of Shakespeare's *King Lear*, Edgar speaks of "the foul fiend Flibbertigibbet," who "hurts the poor creature of earth").

For a time, when the Fat Lady is out of commission, another portrait is in charge, a knight named Sir Cadogan; his passwords include *scurvy cur* and *oddsbodkins*. This last is an exclamation meaning God's body, '*od* being a minced form of *God* (like *gee* for *Jesus*) which came into vogue around 1600. Exclamations of the period included *od's blood, od's body, od's bones, od's wounds*, and so on, which turned into *od's bob, od's bodikins, odsbodlikins, odspittikens, odskilderkins, odzounds*, and so on. (Sir Cadogan, by the way, is a real person in British history. His portrait shows him with hair secured in back by a ribbon. *Cadogan* became the word for this hairstyle.)

In much the same way as these words serve as passwords to gain entrance into the private rooms of Hogwarts, the invented vocabulary and wordplay of the *Harry Potter* books serve as passwords for us Muggles to gain entrance into the wizard world. Someday, perhaps, we will have an annotated version of the *Harry Potter* books (like the annotated *Alice in Wonderland* or *Wizard of Oz*), explaining and expanding on the lexical origins of wizard vocabulary. For now, however, we have to make do with the unwitting collaborative efforts of *Harry Potter* fans all over the world creating websites and writing articles on the subject.

CHAPTER 2

Harry Potter's Place in Literature

READINGS ON
J.K. ROWLING

Real Lessons from a Fantasy World

Roni Natov

J.K. Rowling's success in the *Harry Potter* books results, in part, from her conscious blending of real and fantasy worlds. Unlike many children's fantasy books where the supernatural world is completely separate from the real one, Rowling's world takes place amid the ordinary one of the *Muggles*. In fusing the real and the fantastic, Rowling is able to imply real-world lessons about how children may succeed in an often-hostile environment. Harry Potter is both a real boy and a supernatural one. He must, like all children, learn to deal with his fondest dreams and his darkest fears, and he comes to understand that sharing, building community, and including those who are weak as well as those who are strong, are all important aspects of living in society. In this manner, Rowling uses a magical world to imply real-life lessons about growing into a strong, caring person. Roni Natov teaches English and children's studies at Brooklyn College, CUNY. For many years she coedited the journal, *The Lion and the Unicorn*.

Harry begins his journey at eleven years old, an age associated with coming into consciousness, particularly for boys, and particularly in England, when children begin their "serious" study to prepare them for adult life. What Harry discovers on his eleventh birthday is that he is a wizard, that he has powers he intuits but, as is true of most childhood knowledge, does not consciously recognize. He had noticed that strange things happened to him: his hair grew back overnight after his aunt

Roni Natov, "Harry Potter and the Extraordinariness of Ordinary," *The Lion and the Unicorn*, vol. 25, April 2001, pp. 310–27. Copyright © 2001 by Johns Hopkins University Press. Reproduced by permission.

sheared it off; the sweater she tried to force him to wear kept getting smaller when she tried to pull it over his head. A most hilarious scene occurs at the zoo where the caged boa winks at him, after sleeping through his cousin Dudley's command to "'Make it move,'" and, as it makes its escape amid "howls of horror," Harry "could have sworn a low hissing voice said, 'Brazil, here I come. . . . Thanksss, amigo.'" He does not connect these events with his own power. Like most orphans, Harry has little sense of having any power at all.

Like most orphan heroes, he will need to be unusually sensitive, almost vigilant, particularly since he has been raised by hostile relatives against whom his sensibility absolutely grates. He has to make his own choices, as Rowling pointed out in a National Public Radio (NPR) interview, without the benefit of "access to adults," the "safety net of many children who have loving parents or guardians."

An Orphan on His Own

However extreme this situation, it only epitomizes what I believe at one time every child feels—that she is on her own, unacknowledged, unappreciated, unseen, and unheard, up against an unfair parent, and by extension, an unfair world. Justice and the lack of it reign supreme in the literature of childhood, where our first sense of the world is often so astutely recorded. "But it's not fair" is a phrase that stands out from my childhood and continues to resonate for me even now. I am reminded of E.B. White's opening to the beloved classic, *Charlotte's Web:* "'Where's Poppa going with that axe?'" White's hero, Fern, protests against the adults' Darwinian treatment of animals, those creatures closest to her child-sensibility: "'But it's unfair! . . . The pig couldn't help being born small. . . . If *I* had been very small at birth,'" she accuses, "'would you have killed *me?*'"

And what could be more unfair than losing your parents as a baby? The orphan archetype embodies the childhood task of learning to deal with an unfair world. I am also reminded of [English author Charlotte Brontë's hero] Jane Eyre at ten years old, thrashing around in her awareness of her unjust treatment at the hands of her aunt and cousins. Harry, like his great Victorian predecessors, is a kind of Everychild, vulnerable in his powerlessness, but as he discovers his strengths, he releases a new source of vitality into the world. He becomes the child-hero of his own story, like [English author Charles] Dickens's "favorite child," the orphan hero of *David Copperfield*, whose story begins, "Whether I shall turn out to be the hero of my own life, or whether that station will be held by anybody else, these pages must show." The *Harry Potter* stories chronicle the process of the child's movement from the initial consciousness of himself as the central character in his story, a singular preoccupation with self, to a sense of his own power and responsibility to a larger community.

THE PERFECTLY NORMAL DURSLEYS

Harry Potter has been raised by the Dursleys, who pride themselves on being "perfectly normal"—a sign that this story will assert the unconventional, even the eccentric. Harry will provide a resistance to normality that, Rowling suggests, is necessary for inclusiveness, for the individual and the community to prosper. Mr. Dursley, director of Grunnings, which makes drills, is a brutal, "beefy man with hardly any neck." His equally nasty opposite, Mrs. Dursley, is "thin . . . [with] nearly twice the usual amount of neck . . . [good for] spying on the neighbors." These are the caretakers of "the boy who lived" through the murder of both his parents and the attempt on his own life. Many are the injustices heaped upon him: he is kept under the stairs, half-starved and half-clothed, is "small and skinny for his age . . . [his] glasses held together with a lot of Scotch tape because of all the times Dudley had punched him on the nose." The Dursleys are also psychologically abusive and provide, conversely, a model of how not to treat children. They treat Harry "as though he wasn't there . . . as though he was something very nasty that couldn't understand them, like a slug." They withhold the truth of Harry's birth, in violation of a basic tenet of children's rights—one of the many indications that Rowling sees children as people with rights. What they hate in Harry's behavior, "even more than his asking questions [is] his talking about anything acting in a way it shouldn't, no matter if it was in a dream or even a cartoon." Here Rowling emphasizes the preeminence of the imagination of childhood and the need for children to question and dream. So when Harry dreams of a flying motorcycle, it foreshadows his success at Quidditch, a kind of soccer in the sky, and his imminent rise above the chains of conventionality. Normal, Muggle (non-magical) school is a system that teaches children to use "knobbly sticks for hitting each other . . . [as if it were] good training for later life." There Harry is persecuted by Dudley's "normal" friends, like Piers, "a scrawny boy with a face like a rat . . . who held people's arms behind their backs while Dudley hit them" —because he is different, because he is an orphan, because he is dressed in Dudley's old, shrunken uniforms, "looking like he was wearing bits of old elephant skin. . . ." Aside from his dark cupboard under the stairs, nowhere is Harry safe. And nowhere is he loved, which only provides the urgency for a compensatory endowment of magical powers.

A Special Boy

Belying Harry's puny appearance and weak position in the Muggle world is his bolt-of-lightning scar, which marks him, like Cain [biblical murderer of his brother Abel] for difference and protection against antagonism to that uniqueness. When Harry is most vulnerable, his scar burns painfully, which serves to warn him against proximity of danger. A particularly touching image of Harry's vulnerability occurs at the end of the first chapter, where he is curled fetus-like in sleep, "not knowing he was special, not knowing he was famous . . . that at this very moment, people meeting in secret all over the country were holding up their glasses and saying in hushed voices: 'To Harry Potter—the boy who lived!'"

Harry embodies this state of injustice frequently experienced by children, often as inchoate fear and anger—and its other side, desire to possess extraordinary powers that will overcome such early and deep exile from the child's birthright of love and protection. That every child experiences himself as special is obvious, if for no other reason than that everything that happens to him is inherently significant. The world revolves around him; each moment resonates with the potential vitality of the first time, of unexplored territory. As the child grows into consciousness, an inner world serves to witness the extraordinary quality of experience recorded, sorted through, and reflected upon. Along with this consciousness comes the recognition that others may share that experience, in part at least, and that ultimately each child is just another human being on this large, multitudinous planet. I remember looking up at the stars one night in the country and coming to a sudden understanding that contained both terror and relief. My epiphany turned on how small and insignificant I was, coupled with the insight that I was not responsible for the world. I had only a small part to play; the world was long in the making before I entered it and would go on long after I was gone. I remember that my ordinariness, then, offered a perspective and put into sharp relief my need to be special.

The *Harry Potter* series opens with the infiltration of the ordinary world by the luminous and magical as "a large, tawny owl flutters past the window" unobserved by the blunted Dursleys. Mr. Dursley "noticed the first sign of something peculiar—a cat reading a map," but assumed that "[i]t must have been a trick of the light . . . and put the cat out of his mind." He was aware of "a lot of strangely dressed people . . . in cloaks. Mr. Dursley couldn't bear people who dressed in funny clothes . . . [and] was enraged to see that a couple of them weren't young at all," dismissed them as "people [who] *were* obviously collecting for something [and put] his mind back on drills." He was oblivious to "the owls swooping past in broad daylight, though people down in the street . . . pointed and gazed open-mouthed as owl after owl sped overhead." With this startling image of the nocturnal in bright light, Rowling establishes three groups defined by their response to the magic of the world. The Dursleys represent those who are hostile to anything imaginative, new, unpredictable. The Muggles, who notice the owls but are remote from their magical aura, represent a kind of conventional center. Professor Dumbledore, Head of Hogwarts School of Witchcraft and Wizardry, an old man, whose silver hair and beard "were both long enough to tuck into his belt . . . [who wore] long robes, a purple cloak that swept the ground, and high-heeled, buckled boots," and Professor McGonagall, who has shape-shifted from cat to woman, indicated by her glasses with "exactly the shape of the markings the cat had had around its eyes," embody the childhood world of magic and awe.

In most popular children's fantasies, the magical world is entirely separate from daily life. In C.S. Lewis's *The Lion, the Witch, and the Wardrobe,* for example, entry into the supernatural takes place through a wardrobe at the back of a strange house during the bombings of World War II and represents the child-heroes' escape into a reimagined and revitalized Christian realm. In Madeleine L'Engle's *A Wrinkle in Time* and its successors, *A Wind in the Door* and *A Swiftly Tilting Planet,* the magical world is celestial, in keeping with science fiction and L'Engle's strong religious allegorical allusions. J.R.R. Tolkien's *The Hobbit* and *Lord of the Rings* trilogy take place entirely in a magical world and represent a refuge, an alternative to the real world.

Rowling noted the genius of Lewis and Tolkien, those predecessors with whom she has been frequently compared, but she claimed in the NPR radio interview that she was "doing something slightly different." Though her stories contain the usual global battle between the forces of good and evil, Rowling, I believe, is essentially a novelist, strongest when writing about the real world. Harry has a psychology; his problems need resolution in the real world. Insofar as he is a real child, with little relief at home, at Hogwarts School of Witchcraft and Wizardry, where the supernatural reigns, he is freer to discover his own powers. In Rowling's stories, the interpenetration of the two worlds suggests the way in which we live, not only in childhood, though especially so—on more than one plane, with the life of the imagination and daily life moving in and out of our consciousness. . . .

In the *Harry Potter* books, magic calls attention to the awe and wonder of ordinary life. Rowling ingeniously enhances and amplifies the vitality of ordinary objects. For example, at Hogwarts, the walls are "covered with portraits of old head-masters and headmistresses, all of whom were snoozing gently in their frames." Books bite and argue, "locked together in furious wrestling matches and snapping aggressively.". . . Along with magical wands, cloaks of invisibility, maps that re-produce and mirror actual journeys as they are taking place (like the virtual reality of technology), the things of children's culture—treats such as candy, and kids' own particular kind of humor, such as jokes about bodily fluids—are featured. Some of children readers' favorite aspects of life at Hogwarts include Bertie Bott's Every Flavor Beans, consisting of such flavors as spinach, liver, tripe, grass, sardine, vomit, ear wax, and "even a booger-flavored one." Words themselves suggest the magical power of language to mean, as well as to evoke and connote. Such passwords as "pig snout," "scurvy cur," "oddsbodkin," suggest treasure and mystery. The characters' names are appropriately allusive and inviting. As [author Sharon] Moore points out:

> There are sneaky-sounding s's: Slytherins, Snape, Severus, Sirius and Scabbers. The h's are kind of heroic: Hogwarts, Hedwig, Hermione and Hagrid. The f's are

often unpleasant types: Filch and Flitwick. . . . The names that sound French are usually difficult people: Madam Pince, Madam Pomfrey, and Malfoy.

[American novelist] Alison Lurie noted,

> As in many folk tales, you can often tell a character's character from his or her name, and "Voldemort" neatly combines the ideas of theft, mold, and death. Harry Potter, on the other hand, has a name that suggests not only craftsmanship but both English literature and English history: Shakespeare's Prince Hal and Harry Hotspur, the brave, charming, impulsive heroes of *Henry IV,* and Beatrix Potter, who created that other charming and impulsive classic hero, Peter Rabbit. . . .

HARRY IS BOTH SUPERNATURAL AND ORDINARY

Harry's supernatural powers invite children to imagine beyond the boundaries of their limitations: what if I could see and hear without being seen or heard; what if I could fly; what if I could read another's mind. With his magic cloak, Harry is invisible; with his Nimbus 2000 racing broomstick, he can fly; he can even, in the fourth book, project himself into Dumbledore's siphoned-off thoughts. Also, like every child, Harry is one among many, represented here by the fact that his classmates are also wizards. While he is good at playing Quidditch, he is just an ordinary player at his school work; nor is he particularly insightful in the way he relates to or understands others. His classmate Hermione Granger, the girl with whom Rowling most closely identifies, is smarter and more sensitive. Hermione has the most highly developed sense of justice; even though Harry has freed Dobby, the house-elf, Hermione alone understands the oppression of the house-elves, as they serve their masters without pay, "beaming, bowing, and curtsying." Part of Rowling's genius is the creation of stories about the development of the ordinary boy, as he grows from the start of the series at ten years old to the age of seventeen. There will be one book for each year, Rowling announced in December 1998, with the "hormones kicking in." Gender informs Rowling's vision in that she blends the male questor with the feminized hero of tales of school and home; these stories are relational, psychologically nuanced, and in that sense realistic. . . .

HOGWARTS IS BOTH REALISTIC AND FANTASTIC

Most of the adventures take place at school, seen here as the transitional world situated between childhood and adulthood. It is a liminal [a first stage] space that tests the mettle of the child hero and, like all liminal landscapes, it represents "the not-as-yet-conscious," what is yet-to-be, possibility itself, and chance. A burning question for Harry, who has never fit in, not at home, not at Muggle school, who has never had the chance to experience friendship and all that goes along with it—loyalty, competition, finding a place among peers—is how will he succeed in this home away from home? Particularly when he has never been at home at home?

Situating the train that takes people to Hogwarts at 9¾, between tracks 9 and 10, reinforces the central location of these stories between the earth-bound and magical worlds. As Harry transports himself beyond the boundaries of the real world, between tracks 9 and 10, one can viscerally feel his body brace against the shock, his mind unbelieving, as he breaks through what appears to be a solid barrier, as the imagination may seem to do with real life problems. The school and its various accoutrements epitomize the imagination of childhood and the real concerns of children. In the wizard world, everything is adorned with the magic so that, for example, the point of entry into the bank, a warning against greed and snobbishness—a worldly concern—is heightened by the poetic language on the sign: *Enter, stranger, but take heed / Of what awaits the sin of greed.* . . . There are many such indications of Rowling's abhorrence of the class system, its divisiveness, the negative potential of specialness. Malfoy, the pale boy with the pointed face, whose sense of self is based on embracing his father's money and social position, is early established as Harry's enemy, just as Ron Weasley, who has to share the little his family has with his six siblings, and Hermione, the racially mixed daughter of a Muggle and a wizard, are his best friends.

While Hogwarts contains all the offensive and irritating aspects of real life—it in fact mirrors its elitism and petty power struggles—it is also a wondrous and humorous world. Required reading, for example, abounds with hilarious matches, such as: *One Thousand Magical Herbs and Fungi* by Phyllida Spore and *Fantastic Beasts and Where to Find Them* by Newt Scamader. The magical Sorting Hat matches each child with her proper house (Harry and his friends are assigned to Gryffindor for their courage) and wands intricately fit their owners. The phoenix that provided the feathers for Harry's wand did the same for Voldemort, the "brother [who] gave you that scar," Harry is told, linking him, as Lucifer was God's fallen angel, to his dark enemy. And there is much darkness in these books. However, it is always rooted in the psychological darkness associated with childhood and with human development: with anger, loss, death, grief, fear, and with desire. Although initially Harry is elated when he hears the news of his powers, he is also alarmed and bewildered. Hagrid notes that it's hard to be singled out, and Harry protests, "'Everyone thinks I'm special . . . but I don't know anything about magic at all. . . . I can't even remember what I'm famous for.'" Fear of his power, unsure of how to control desire, or how to recognize and use his gifts wisely— Harry, as Everychild, needs guidance.

THE MIRROR: WHAT CHILDREN DREAM OF

Rowling is adept at providing paradigms for thoughtful, courageous, and moral behavior for children, with clear explanations of the states of feeling that accompany the process. These deeper moments of reflection serve as pauses in the rapid pace of these page-turners. It seems to me that the best mysteries, adventure stories, and romances represent a negotiation between the reckless pace of the narrative breathlessly moving forward and the meditative pockets that provide the space and time to turn inward—to affirm our sense that something memorable is happening to us, something we can retrieve for later, after the book is ended. As is true of our best writers, Rowling draws these opposing realms so seamlessly that they appear to have always been there, side by side, the event and its meaning exquisitely illuminated.

In the first book, *Harry Potter and the Sorcerer's Stone*, the scene in which Harry comes upon the Mirror of Erised (thinly disguised so children will discover that it represents desire) and sees, for the first time in his life, his family, "he had a powerful kind of ache inside him, half joy, half terrible sadness." How fascinating that his friend Ron sees only himself decked out as Head Boy, his own "deepest, most desperate desire." Ron, whose strongest wish is to stand out from his five brothers and from Harry as well, assumes he is seeing the future, just as Harry believed he was looking into his past. However, this mirror, says Dumbledore, "will give us neither knowledge or truth." It can drive us mad, "not knowing if what it shows is real or even possible." He warns against "dwell[ing] in dreams" as one could "forget to live." However, he offers, "If you ever *do* run across it, you will now be prepared.". . . At its core, Rowling suggests, desire can be both alluring and dangerous. Children need to understand, on whatever level, its complexity. Rowling does not minimize childhood longing. She offers this small allegory with the understanding that the search for identity is reflected in that mirror—as Harry sees his family behind him and desires only to return again and again to that vision of himself, supported by those who resemble him, smiling at and waving to him. This scene prepares for the ones that follow, in which Harry comes into deeper and darker knowledge, though always returning to this central issue of identity and the protection it promises.

BOGGARTS: WHAT CHILDREN FEAR

If the Mirror reflects what we most long for, it also evokes the fear that accompanies such desire and the loss that engendered it. In *Harry Potter and the Prisoner of Azkaban*, Rowling focuses on this fear, beginning with the boggarts who take the shape of "whatever each of us most fears." For Harry, as his Dark Arts teacher tells him, it is fear itself, embodied in the dementors, the prison guards of Azkaban. What tortures Harry is his overwhelming guilt and sorrow at his mother's death. At the sight of these grey-hooded figures, Harry hears his mother's desperate cries: "'No, take me, kill me instead.'" Haunted by her pain and guilty that she died to save him, Harry is drawn into intense ambivalence, which Rowling explains:

> Terrible though it was to hear his parents' last moments replayed inside his head, these were the only times Harry had heard their voices since he was a very small child. . . ."They're dead," he told himself sternly . . ."and listening to echoes of them won't bring them back. You'd better get a grip on yourself if you want that Quidditch Cup."

The desire to be reunited with his parents, though natural and inevitable, serves as a warning, as with the Mirror, against remaining in the past, lost in memory or desire. Of course, in addition to exploring Harry's inner demons, here Rowling connects despair with madness and suggests that it is the loss of hope that makes us demented, that promotes criminality and destroys the heart. The dementors, those who are supposed to guard prisoners,

> drain peace, hope, and happiness out of the air around them. Get too near a dementor and every good feeling, every happy memory will be sucked out of you. . . .

> [S]oul-less and evil . . . you'll be left with nothing but
> the worst experiences of your life. . . . [S]et on a tiny
> island, way out to sea . . . they don't need walls and wa-
> ter to keep the prisoners in, not when they're all
> trapped inside their heads, incapable of a single cheer-
> ful thought. Most of them go mad within weeks.

The antidote for such haunting is happy memories, those
that make children feel safe, loved, confident, good about
themselves. More than anything, a sense of self is exactly
what Hagrid was denied in prison, as he tells Harry: "'Yeh
can really remember who yeh are after a while.'" Knowing
who you are is at the heart here, the development of the
child's consciousness, the narrative of Everychild—the right
to knowledge and expression of self. . . .

BEYOND A SIMPLE CONCEPT OF EVIL

Children are also led beyond the simple concept of evil as
purely bad guys whose struggles abound in the earlier books.
With the third volume, *Harry Potter and the Prisoner of Azkaban*, what appears evil turns out to be a paradoxical figure,
Lupin, who is a werewolf, a force of good that can be dangerous as well. . . . What is most interesting here is that the
potentially destructive part of the werewolf is humanized
and offered with understanding. Rowling establishes his innocence and evokes compassion for him, as he tells his story.
Lupin says, "'I was a very small boy when I received the bite.
My parents tried everything, but in those days there was no
cure. . . . My transformations . . . were terrible. It is very
painful to turn into a werewolf. I was separated from humans to bite, so I bit and scratched myself instead.'" As
Lupin becomes a werewolf when he doesn't take his potion,
madness and self-destructive impulses are depicted with a
kind of psychological truth. Rowling attempts to humanize
the demonic, rather than demonize the human.

The servants of evil are recognizable as frail humans who
have grown large because they are adults who are out of con-

trol—what is often most terrifying to children. Peter Petti-grew, in *Harry Potter and the Prisoner of Azkaban*, is "horrible to watch, like an oversized, balding baby, cowering on the floor," and Voldemort, who represents the generating power of evil, the force of discord and enmity, bears "the shape of a crouched human child, except Harry had never seen anything less like a child. It was hairless and scaly-looking. . . . Its arms and legs were thin and feeble, and its face—no child alive ever had a face like that. . . . The thing seemed almost helpless; it raised its thin arms, put them around Wormtail's neck, and Wormtail lifted it." The infantile adult, a kind of perverted innocence, childish without anything childlike, is most hor-rifying when, as a child, it is the controlling force of your life.

CHILDREN TAKING CONTROL

How children take control of their lives—most crucial and central here—is metaphorically represented in several ways. Harry and Hermione watch themselves in "a Time-Turner," able to replay an event, to be in more than one place at a time, to go back in time while remaining in the present, to redo their mistakes and save the lovely hippogriff, Buckbeak. Harry tells Hermione, "'I knew I could do it this time . . . because I'd already done it. . . . Does that make sense?'"—ex-pressing the paradoxical sense of knowing what we didn't know we knew. Even more psychologically profound is the way in which Rowling demonstrates what can be retrieved, even in the final loss of the death of a parent. To protect him-self from fear, Harry conjures up a "Patronus," an image of his father. As an orphan, Harry will have to provide for him-self the father he has never known. Here is a kind of child vi-sion of father atonement. Dumbledore, in such a vision as a father figure, tells Harry: "'You think the dead we loved ever truly leave us? You think that we don't recall them more clearly than ever in times of great trouble? Your father is alive in you, Harry, . . . you did see [him] last night. . . . You found him inside yourself.'" . . .

The *Harry Potter* stories center on what children need to find internally—the strength to do the right thing, to establish a moral code. As hero, Harry must go beyond the apparent truth of things and, ultimately, learn to trust what he sees and act on what is right. The tournament of the fourth volume, *Harry Potter and the Goblet of Fire*, departs from the rather simple victory of Quidditch tournaments, where one house at Hogwarts beats the others, Harry serving as Seeker, the primary position, for Gryffindor. In this book, as Hermione points out, "'This whole tournament's supposed to be about getting to know foreign wizards and making friends with them.'" Although Ron with partial truth responds, "'No it isn't. It's about winning,'" more is at stake here. The community is larger, more global. What it means to "win" is interrogated. In an expansive leap of feeling, Harry saves his rivals, along with his friends. Voices tell him: "'Your task is to retrieve your own friend . . . leave the others. . . .'" He wonders, "Why hadn't he just grabbed Ron and gone? He would have been first back. . . . Cedric and Krum hadn't wasted time worrying about anyone else. . . ." In response, he resists such individualism with "'an equally strong bond of friendship and trust. Differences of habit and language are nothing at all,'" Dumbledore tells him, "'if our aims are identical and our hearts are open.'" Harry and his closest rival, Cedric (who took Cho Chang, the object of Harry's desire, to the ball) help and support each other, and finally decide to reach the Cup at the same time, thus producing two winners. While Cedric dies, and thus Harry alone bears the reward, the boys' rejection of the school's either/or policy establishes a new paradigm of sharing, building community, and inclusiveness.

Harry Potter Is a Fairy Tale

Richard Bernstein

In this article, Richard Bernstein theorizes about the reasons *Harry Potter* is so compelling to children and so ordinary to many adults. To answer this question, Bernstein cites child psychologist Bruno Bettelheim and his landmark study of fairy tales, *The Uses of Enchantment*. In this study Bettelheim wrote that fairy tales enable children to deal with the harsh realities of life in a less threatening environment, that of fiction. Bernstein suggests that the *Harry Potter* books serve a similar function for today's children, in that they contain many of the familiar patterns found in fairy tales, and children who read them find solace in knowing that, at the end of the struggle, the hero will always emerge victorious. Richard Bernstein has served as a book critic for the *New York Times*, and as *Time* magazine's Beijing, China, bureau chief. His books include *Asia: From the Center of the Earth* and *Ultimate Journey*.

It was a quarter of a century ago that Bruno Bettelheim, the child psychologist, accounted for what may be the most impressive and otherwise mysterious publishing phenomenon of the season: the fact that the Harry Potter mysteries by the previously unknown J.K. Rowling are turning out to be among the best-selling books in history.

In his classic study of children's literature, *The Uses of Enchantment*, Bettelheim denigrated most children's books as mere entertainments, lacking in psychological meaning. The great exception to this rule was fairy tales, to which Bettelheim attributed something close to magical power. "More can be learned from them about the inner problems of human beings," he wrote, "and of the right solutions to their predicaments in any society than from any other type of story within a child's comprehension."

That was quite a statement at the time, applied as it was to a form of literature that depicted fantastical worlds, seemed unnecessarily scary, depended on unrealistically happy endings and had very little claim on high literary culture.

FAIRY TALES EXPLAIN THE REAL WORLD

But Bettelheim's main idea was that children live with greater terrors than most adults can understand, and fairy tales both give uncanny expression to that terror and show a way to a better future. The same can be said of the Harry Potter books, and that could well be the reason why the three published so far [1999] occupy the first, second and third places on the *New York Times* hardcover fiction best-seller list, something that no other author in living memory has achieved before.

Ms. Rowling's books are not fairy tales in the conventional Grimm Brothers sense, and they are not as good either. They lack the primal, brutal terror of the Grimm stories, and it was the expression given to that terror that was at the heart of their emotional usefulness for Bettelheim. The Harry Potter stories are light, modern tales, Indiana Jones–like fantasies for children.

When I began to read them, having heard how great they were from my several addicted nephews, it was hard for me to understand what all the sensation was about. Conservative Christians have criticized the Harry Potter books, saying they lead their young readers in the direction of paganism. For me the problem was that Ms. Rowling's world of sorcerers, gravity-defying broomsticks, spells, potions, unicorns and centaurs, goblins, trolls, three-headed dogs and other monstrous and magical creations seemed so divorced from any reality as to kill off the narrative excitement.

But whereas adults see in Harry Potter a fairly conventional supernatural adventure story—one not nearly as brilliant or literary as, say, "The Hobbit" or the "Alice in Wonderland" books—something more fundamental evidently reverberates in the minds of children, something as powerful as the witch of "Hansel and Gretel." And read from this point of view, the Harry Potter books do indeed contain many of the elements that Bettelheim identified in the Grimm tales. Ms. Rowling's success in this sense may show the continued power of the form and the archetypes that those long-ago Germans perfected.

THE HERO AS A KEY FACTOR

The key here is, not surprisingly, the hero, Harry himself, who is 10 years old in Ms. Rowling's first book. One of the first things we learn about him is that his parents died when he was an infant; he is being raised by an aunt and uncle who are dumb, stiff and uncomprehending and who treat him with stingy cruelty. Following Bettelheim's model, this would be very similar to the archetype of the evil stepmother as a representative of the "bad" parent who frighteningly and uncontrollably replaces the "good" parent. What children see at the outset in the Harry Potter books is a lonely boy being raised by evil people, and all parents seem evil to their children at least some of the time.

Unknown to Harry is that his real mother and father, who died when he was a baby, were important sorcerers who were killed by a certain Voldemort, the evil genius of this story, who has been trying to seize power for eons. Here Ms. Rowling's adventure takes on a primal quality that links it with many classic tales, from "Great Expectations" to "Star Wars": there are a family secret and a family struggle passed down from one generation to another, and a lot of meaning comes when the true nature of that struggle is revealed.

What is important in the fairy tale scheme is that Harry's situation contains many of the inchoate [unformed; beginning] fears of childhood, not just the parental abandonment fear. Harry is skinny and weak and wears glasses patched together with tape, and in this sense he seems to stand in for the vulnerability, the powerlessness that children feel. He lives in a cupboard under the stairs, since his spoiled cousin has both of the children's bedrooms upstairs, so in a sense he is expelled, like Hansel and Gretel, even from the evil home he has.

THE CINDERELLA THEME

Most conspicuously, Harry is picked on by his cousin, Dudley, the son of Harry's guardians, who treat Dudley with blatant favoritism. There could hardly be a stronger echo of another common fairy tale theme, exemplified by Cinderella's evil stepsisters.

To Bettelheim the conflict between Cinderella and her stepsisters represents the intense sibling rivalries that children feel and the fears that these rivalries give rise to. Fairy tales, with their eventual happy endings, point a way out for the child who otherwise, Bettelheim said, has no hope "that he will be rescued, that those who he is convinced despise him and have power over him will come to recognize his superiority."

In the early stages of Harry's story the disadvantages he feels are partly recapitulated outside his home. After he learns that he is somebody, the son of famous sorcerers, Harry goes off to Hogwart's School of Witchcraft and Wizardry. There he discovers that other students all seem to know more than he does, that they are insiders while he is the quintessential outsider.

One boy in particular is the head of a small gang that picks on him. A teacher seems intensely and for no reason to dislike him. But gradually Harry emerges as an independent figure whose talents and skills are widely recognized. The rest of Ms. Rowling's first volume shows Harry assuming his true identity, gaining the courage to overcome obstacles and winning a battle against the adversaries of his ancestors.

ASSURANCE OF SUCCESS

Harry's story, in other words, with its early images of alienation, rejection, loneliness and powerlessness leading to its classically fairy tale ending, contains the same basic message that Bettelheim described in "The Uses of Enchantment." It is "that a struggle against severe difficulties in life is unavoidable, is an intrinsic part of human existence—but that if one does not shy away, but steadfastly meets unexpected and often unjust hardships, one masters all obstacles and at the end emerges victorious."

"Morality is not the issue in these tales," Bettelheim said, "but rather, assurance that one can succeed." Such assurance comes in ways that adults often do not understand, but Ms. Rowling's Harry Potter seems to provide it.

Harry Potter and Stoic Philosophy

Edmund Kern

Writing as a historian, Edmund Kern sees links between the *Harry Potter* books and the need for stoic philosophy in an age of catastrophic world events. The notorious terrorist attacks of September 11, 2001, raised the need for a new kind of fortitude among children and adults alike, and this same trait of stoic philosophy is found prominently in the *Harry Potter* series. Kern presents a brief history of Stoicism and an overview of its philosophical tenets to suggest that Harry Potter provides a model of how to deal with adversity in his adoption of a stoic attitude toward events that are out of his control. Harry's struggles attract both children and adults who must come to terms with the often tragic world in which we live. His struggle can be a lesson to all of us about just what is really important in life. Edmund Kern has served as a professor of history at Lawrence University in Appleton, Wisconsin. His primary interests include early modern Europe, religious culture, the Habsburgs, and Austria.

Critics of the expanding Potter empire claim to have the best interests of children at heart. They believe that J.K. Rowling, the author of the Potter books, is promoting dangerous ideas that could lead young minds astray or (at best) writing clever books that contribute to a rampant culture of consumerism. But the attacks on the morality of the Potter series are misplaced.

Focusing on the books themselves shows that Rowling develops an essentially Stoic moral philosophy through the ethical dilemmas in which she places Harry and his friends—

Edmund Kern, "Harry Potter, Stoic Boy Wonder," *The Chronicle of Higher Education*, November 16, 2001, pp. B18–19. Copyright © 2001 by Edmund Kern. Reproduced by permission.

dilemmas requiring them to think in complex ways about right and wrong. Her version of Stoicism is admittedly an updated one, but nonetheless one whose chief virtue is old-fashioned constancy. Harry's resolution in the face of adversity is the result of conscious choice and attention to what is and is not within his control. Harry worries about who he is, but realizes that what he does matters most. And, I believe, so do the children reading the books.

But children aren't the only ones absorbed by the adventures of Harry Potter. Adults have been enchanted as well. In some ways, Rowling tells a typical coming-of-age story, but in presenting Harry and his friends, she has measured the sensibilities of today's kids. They see the constraints placed upon them but value their own decision making. Perhaps it is this same formula that appeals to adults reading the books. The works tap into a philosophy that offers comfort to readers—both children and adults—as they try to work their ways through the uncertainty of the world.

HARRY CONFRONTS THE UGLINESS OF LIFE

Recent events have only intensified the need for comfort. The terrorist assaults of September 11 [2001] and subsequent attacks with anthrax spores have replaced vague feelings of insecurity with the promise of future threats. Yet unease and fear are being met with calls for resolve, vigilance, patience, and justice—Stoic responses for governing the emotional reactions of anger, panic, rash behavior, and a desire for vengeance.

Harry Potter comes to face similarly intensified threats. As his world becomes increasingly uncertain, he finds guidance but no easy way out of his predicament.

Although in interviews Rowling claims not to be writing for any particular audience, her brilliance shows most clearly in the authorial voice she adapts for each book, which matures along with Harry. Rowling's voice speaks to children, rather than at them. They thus encounter the chicken-blood-and-brandy diet of baby dragons, vomit-flavored candy, and (mildly) off-color jokes, along with occasional drunkenness and violence. Life is not pristine. The death of a likable, righteous character proves that acting morally is hard and that being good does not guarantee being rewarded.

The frankness in the Potter books liberates children. Rather than smothering young readers, it presents an appealing ethic that they can both relate to and think through. Harry and his friends are not above giving into temptation, breaking the rules, or even acting contrary to explicit instruction. Yet their chief motives are empathy, compassion, and tolerance, virtues mostly absent, in contrast, from [writer and former U.S. secretary of education] William J. Bennett's preachy *The Children's Book of Virtues.* Despite occasional misbehavior, the characters remain steadfast in an ongoing battle between good and evil.

Harry senses that he has some frightful enemies and that he is the target of vengeance. Despite some cheery optimism, he has a pronounced sense of fatalism [belief that all events are determined by fate]. It is easy to underestimate how appealing this is to young readers whose lives turn on the whims of others, and how satisfying it is to follow a character working his way through difficult circumstances. (Even adults, ostensibly more in control of their own lives, have no difficulty identifying with those themes.) Even though events are beyond Harry's control, he is governed ultimately by rules of his own making. In precisely this way, Rowling introduces the Stoicism so central to the moral system at work in her series.

THE VALUE OF STOICISM

Harry Potter's morality is not unlike that on display in the works of [English fantasy novelists] J.R.R. Tolkien, C.S. Lewis, or most recently Philip Pullman, where Stoic constancy is valued. In fact, forms of Stoicism seem to be central to much modern children's literature. Perhaps that is not surprising. Our era has witnessed both extreme mass violence and the wearing away of objective epistemologies. An updated Stoicism provides guidance, without advancing a new orthodoxy, in the midst of so much uncertainty—as Harry Potter's fans seem to recognize.

Here Rowling follows the same path as other authors of children's literature. Tolkien, Lewis, and Pullman each show how self-control, in service of a larger good, is the only sure means of being true to the self and securing the victory. In each of these authors' works, even though characters never offer up a universal distinction between good and evil, they know the difference when they see it. That difference depends on the ability to imagine the suffering of others and to do something about it. Withdrawal from empathy signals the advent of evil.

Again, the events of September 11 seem germane to assessing the appeal of Rowling's ethical system. A common response to televised horror was shock—a shock prompted not only by the audacity of the attacks, but also by the terrorists' perceived inability to associate their acts with enormous suffering among both victims and survivors. An outpouring of support—shared grief, volunteerism, and charitable contributions—alleviated the shock and restored an imaginative, empathetic connection to those harmed by the attacks. In the minds of many, even such limited denial of the self became an opportunity for acting on behalf of an apparent greater good.

A Brief History of Stoicism

In the midst of violent political turmoil in 1584, as Spain sought to put down the revolt of the United Provinces in the Netherlands, the philosopher Justus Lipsius asked what was the proper response of the thinking person to adverse circumstances. The result became his neo-Stoic [or new Stoic] classic, *The Book of Constancy.* As his title suggests, Lipsius found the answer in "a right and immovable strength of mind, neither lifted up nor pressed down with external or casual accidents." Such steadfastness was to stem from sound reason, found internally but corresponding to the true nature of things. Thinking persons were to make their will correspond to what was right (understood by the Christian Lipsius as the will of God). In adverse circumstances, they endured rather than seeking to flee.

Stoicism has a long history, beginning in the fourth century B.C.E. [Before the Common Era]. An important school of thought since then, its most famous proponents are [ancient Roman philosophers] Seneca and Marcus Aurelius. It affected the thought of Renaissance humanists and Christian reformers alike, spreading its influence well into the 20th century.

Today, both Christian thinkers and the more secular-minded make use of the basic elements of Stoic thinking. The former invoke a transcendent God who is not only all-powerful but caring. The latter (a more diverse group) emphasize the solidarity of all humans, the primacy of reason, the need for self-sacrifice, or the interconnectedness of things (particularly in relation to environmental matters). . . .

STOICISM EXPLAINED

According to the Stoics, living well means living in accord with the world, which divine reason has shaped. Nature (or the divine within it) is thus the standard for the regulation of life; it not only dictates proper action but also dictates the outcome of events. In practical terms, fate consists of things beyond a person's control. Within this scheme, Stoics distinguish among good things (virtues, virtuous acts, good feelings), bad things (vices, vicious acts, bad feelings), and indifferent things—which are further divided into preferred things (e.g., life, beauty, health) or rejected things (e.g., death, ugliness, illness).

Stoics embrace what is good, deplore what is bad, and either value or discount what is indifferent. Stoicism seeks to subject internal desires, feelings, and even judgments to restraints that cultivate the self in service of a greater good. Virtue results only from conscious choice and attention to what is within one's control.

Although Rowling is careful not to present that version of Stoicism explicitly, she introduces the basic ideas in her first book. Her characters may value life and material possessions, but they realize that many things are more important. Professor Dumbledore explains the folly in Voldemort's search for the philosopher's stone:

"After all, to the well-organized mind, death is but the next great adventure. You know, the Stone was really not such a wonderful thing. As much money and life as you could want! The two things most human beings would choose above all—the trouble is, humans do have a knack of choosing precisely those things which are worst for them."

Even Rowling's younger readers, who may be only dimly aware of violence, prejudice, and class antagonism in the real world, can respond to the books' Stoic appeal for responsibility. Harry Potter becomes familiar with evil, and he learns how to cope with it—remaining true to what is right regardless of consequence. He remains constant. My local librarian tells me that children often point to a key passage in which Harry worries about who he is. When Dumbledore says "it's our choices, Harry, that show what we truly are, far more than our abilities," he knows intimately that Harry has already demonstrated as much. The children reading the books do as well. Drawn to his magical world and won over by his qualities, they want to emulate Harry Potter.

Walt Disney used to speak of the "four C's" as essential to realizing dreams: curiosity, confidence, courage, and constancy. Wait a minute. Constancy? Yes. Take a look at Harry Potter and find it anew. The kids in your life already have.

I had originally planned to end my remarks there—with a glib observation linking Harry Potter's popularity to the Stoic themes manifest in his actions. It's not an uncommon formula, after all. But in the shadows cast by the events of September 11, it has taken on a new significance. Simple Stoic fortitude may not be the answer to our current plight, but it is certainly one in which many have found solace.

The Sources of *Harry Potter*

Wendy Doniger

Wendy Doniger is a comparative mythologist, a scholar
who studies and compares the myths of a variety of cultures. In this essay she applies her expertise to the *Harry
Potter* novels and derives three major genres, or types of
stories, that inform J.K. Rowling's series. Doniger first
cites what psychologist Sigmund Freud called the "family
saga," often depicted as an orphaned hero's struggle to deal
with an adoptive family after his own parents have been
killed. The second type of story is the boys' boarding
school tale, a well-known English genre in which issues of
class often cause conflict for the main character. A third
genre Rowling uses is that of fantasy, and Rowling's particular type of fantasy story is one where magic is quite ordinary. Doniger suggests that Rowling weaves these three
types of well-known stories together, with creative genius,
to form the *Harry Potter* books. Rowling takes elements
from a variety of other stories and combines them to come
up with a brilliant new creation: the adventures of a magical, orphaned boarding school boy named Harry Potter.
Wendy Doniger has taught at the University of Chicago.
Among her long list of books are *Other Peoples' Myths: The
Cave of Echoes* (1995), *The Implied Spider: Politics and
Theology in Myth* (1998), and *Splitting the Difference: Gender and Myth in Ancient Greece and India* (1999).

Young Harry Potter's parents are dead. So far, so good: many
of the heroes and heroines of the classics of children's literature are orphans, while others have invisible, unmentionable
or irrelevant parents. The sorrow of grieving, not to mention

Wendy Doniger, "Spot the Source: Harry Potter Explained," www.books.guardian.
co.uk, February 10, 2000. Copyright © 2000 by London Review of Books, Ltd.
Reprinted with permission.

the terror of helplessness, is quickly glossed over in favour of the joy of a fantasised freedom. (A particularly sharp 13-year-old patiently explained to me that if Harry's parents weren't dead, there would be no point in writing the book: it wouldn't be interesting, no matter how many creative details there were.)

The problem, for Harry Potter as for most orphans in children's books, is not the absence of parents but the presence of step-parents. From infancy Harry has been raised by his horrid Uncle Vernon and Aunt Petunia Dursley, who hate him and dote on their own cruel and stupid son, Dudley Dursley; they starve Harry and, when he's forced to spend summer holidays with them, they intercept his letters from his school friends, his only link with the world of people who care for him.

THE FAMILY ROMANCE

Harry's dead parents, Lily and James, were not ordinary humans but a powerful witch and wizard. The Dursleys seldom speak about them, and when they do it's always with contempt, but as Harry grows up he begins to learn about them and to learn that he, too, is a wizard, though he is not (generally) allowed to use his powers in the world of the Muggles, as the witches and wizards call unmagical humans. This aspect of the story is familiar from mythological literature. [American novelist] Alison Lurie, praising the Harry Potter books in the New York Review of Books, saw in them 'the common childhood fantasy that the dreary adults and siblings you live with are not your real family, that you are somehow special and gifted'.

[Psychologist Sigmund] Freud called this the Family Romance and argued for its utility in defining your apparent parents as people whom (unlike your real parents) you are allowed to desire or hate. This is the Oedipal configuration, best known from the eponymous case that Freud wrote about, but also from the myth of the birth of the hero explored by Freud's disciple Otto Rank. The child's joyful expectation of coming someday into the greatness of his parents sustains him in the present situation of humiliation and impotence.

The sign of Harry's greatness is a scar on his forehead, where a lightning bolt hurled by the evil wizard Voldemort hit him when he was still a baby, and would have killed him but for his mother's self-sacrificial intervention; the scar functions, like the mark of Cain [biblical murderer of his brother Abel; God placed a mark on him for this crime] to set Harry apart. (The evil upper-form [upper grade in British school] boy Malfoy calls him 'Scarhead'.)

The Family Romance haunts the story of the ugly duckling, raised among scornful ducks until he discovers that he's really a swan. It haunts real-life adoption, too, fuelling the obsessive search for biological parents, and part of it (the rags-to-riches Cinderella part) shapes the real-life story of JK Rowling, who rose out of obscurity and deprivation to claim her literary sovereignty. Rowling has been praised for what Lurie and others regard as a particularly British talent for writing for children, but the story she tells is widespread in other cultures too: the birth of [Persian king] Cyrus in [Greek historian] Herodotus, of Krishna and Karna [great heroes] in the Hindu tradition, not to mention Superman in American comics.

Rowling brings new life to the old chestnut. At the end of the first book, Harry learns from the good wizard Dumbledore why Voldemort's successor could not kill him: 'Love as powerful as your mother's leaves its own mark. Not a scar, no visible sign . . . to have been loved so deeply, even though the person who loved us is gone, will give us some protection for ever.' In the second book, Harry explains this protection to the revenant Voldemort: 'You couldn't kill me . . . because my mother died to save me.' In the third book, Harry is haunted by his mother's dying screams, but now that he is older he moves on, in Lacanian fashion [as described by

French psychiatrist Jacques Lacan], to come to terms with his father.

Thanks to a wonderfully complex and subtle episode of time travel that traces a Möbius twist [a strip of material twisted 180 degrees and attached end to end] in the chronological sequence, Harry encounters himself in the loop where past and present come together and overlap. The first time he lives through this period, he sees, across a lake, someone he vaguely recognises: perhaps his father? No, his father is dead, but that person sends a silver stag which saves him from present danger.

When he goes back in time, he runs to the same place to see who it was, and there's no one else there: he is the one who sends the stag to save himself in the future. The moment when Harry realises that he mistook himself for his father is quite powerful; and it is, after all, the only real kind of time travel there is. Each of us becomes, in adulthood, someone who lived some thirty years before us, someone who must save our own life.

THE BOYS' BOARDING SCHOOL

The Family Romance is just one part of Harry's story; it is embedded in a familiar, very English setting, the boys' boarding school. Harry is sent to Hogwarts School of Witchcraft and Wizardry, where he has strange and dangerous adventures, makes friends, and is happy for the first time in his life. Hogwarts is a modern version of the classical boarding school, now co-ed but only superficially multiracial—and still classically francophobe (all the villains have French names). There are passing references to a girl named Parvati Patel and to one black boy; and no Jewish names.

Class, rather than race or religion, is the central issue, and sometimes makes Hogwarts seem like a public school of the Thirties [1930s]: Harry, who is poor in the Muggle world (his glasses are mended with tape), though he has secret deposits of gold in the magic world, is taunted by the rich, snobbish, cowardly, cruel Malfoy, who is backed by his powerful, manipulative father and talks a lot of proto-Nazi drivel about pure blood. But the true epoch of Hogwarts is medieval: it teaches things like Potions, Transfiguration and Defence against the Dark Arts (a hard post to keep filled).

THE ORDINARINESS OF MAGIC

Besides the Family Romance and the schooldays genre, Rowling weaves in a third inherited theme: what might be called the banality of magic. This is magic which is used not to slay dragons or turn men into swine but to slide up the banister (as Mary Poppins does) or to light fires instantly in damp weather (as the Hogwarts wizards do). Harry is told that people who read without permission a book called Sonnets of a Sorcerer are cursed to speak in limericks for the rest of their lives, and there's a charm to demist your glasses in the rain (which proves to be of crucial use for Harry during a Quidditch match on a foul day). There's also a clock that, instead of saying the hours and minutes, says: 'You're late,' and 'Time to make tea.'

Hogwarts is reached by a train that leaves from Platform 9¾ at King's Cross, visible only to people who know where to look for it. The ceiling in the school dining hall is a constantly changing lifelike simulation of the sky, and the portraits are alive: they visit one another and talk to the people outside the frames. Though games loom large, the game of Quidditch is played in the air on flying broomsticks. (For most American children, upper-form boys treating the lower forms as slaves will seem even weirder than people flying around on broomsticks.)

Life at Hogwarts is very different from the life Harry is condemned to live with the Dursleys, but not all that different from the Muggle world in general. The social situations are the same; the people are just the same; and the tasks are the same—go to classes, do homework, pass exams. All that's different is the extended powers of people at Hogwarts, which are not unlike the powers imagined in futuristic novels. Hogwarts is in our world, but pieces of magic are studded in it here and there, almost at random. The line between the magic and non-magic worlds is further blurred when magic is used in the Muggle world. This happens more often than you might think (some Muggle-baiters amuse themselves by putting spells on Muggles' keys so that they shrink to nothing and can't be found), but a Forgetfulness potion is always used to wipe out all record of it.

Rowling handles quite well the inconsistency that follows from having magic forbidden in some situations and allowed in others; a Hogwarts nurse can mend broken bones overnight, but no one can fix a magic broomstick when it shatters on a tree. The line between the things that you can and cannot change (as in time travel) might seem arbitrary. Why not just use magic to get all the answers right in exams? Because it's no fun that way; so the quill pens used in exams are bewitched with an Anti-Cheating spell. This is magic played according to Hoyle [official game rules, after British writer on games Edmund Hoyle], with one hand—the narrative hand—tied behind its back.

THE COMBINATION OF THREE GENRES WORKS WONDERS

The fact that the Harry Potter books are an amalgam of at least three familiar genres works for, not against, their spectacular success. Myths survive for centuries, in a succession of incarnations, both because they are available and because they are intrinsically charismatic. Rowling is a wizard herself at the magic art of bricolage: new stories crafted out of recycled pieces of old stories. As I began to read the books, my inner child, as they say, steeped in children's classics joined forces with my adult self, a comparative mythologist [one who studies myths from a range of cultures], and I found myself unable to resist playing the game of 'Can You Spot the Source?', a philologist's [one who studies literature] variant on the old children's game of 'How Many Animals Can

You Find Hiding in This Picture?' (there was always a stag in the trees, whose branches were his antlers).

I found the Family Romance of [English hero] King Arthur, particularly as reincarnated in [English writer] TH White's Sword in the Stone, in the magic weapon that no one but Harry can wield, and in the gift of talking to animals that White's Merlin gives to Arthur (Harry just does snakes). Where Mary Poppins gave the children a medicine that tasted different for each of them (each one's favourite taste), Rowling gives us Every Flavour Beans, always a surprise. The talking chess pieces from Through the Looking-Glass appear here as small pieces on a conventional board, but they talk back when you move them: 'Don't send me there, can't you see his knight? Send him, we can afford to lose him.'

Snow White's talking mirror appears, but Rowling transforms it both with humour (the mirror over the mantelpiece shouts at Harry, 'Tuck your shirt in, scruffy!' and whispers, 'You're fighting a losing battle there, dear,' when he attempts to plaster down his cowlick) and with something deeper: there is a mirror that shows you your heart's desire (Harry imagines his mother, 'a very pretty woman . . . her eyes are just like mine,' and his father, whose hair 'stuck up at the back, just as Harry's did'). And where both Peter Pan and Mary Poppins taught children to fly or float by thinking happy thoughts, Rowling takes the concept into a more sinister area.

Harry learns that the only way to defend himself against the Dementors, who will destroy him by assuming the form of what he most fears, is by mentally conjuring up a Patronus, 'a projection of the very things that the Dementor feeds upon—hope, happiness, the desire to survive'; and he overpowers one Dementor by imagining life with a loving figure who has offered to adopt him. After a while, however, the collage began to transcend its piecemeal sources, and I stopped playing the philologist's game. But children who do not read—and much of the dancing in the streets celebrating Rowling's success comes from the fact that most of the Harry

Potter crowd are allegedly converted hardcore television and video-game addicts—will here encounter the charisma of [fantasy writers] Lewis, Carroll, Barrie, Tolkien, Nesbitt and Travers, not to mention [English novelists Charles] Dickens and [Robert Louis] Stevenson, all at once.

Comic Genius, Whimsy, and Satire

The old themes are continually fleshed out with touches of comic genius. There are child-pleasing scenes of mayhem, as when the pixies get loose in the Defence against the Dark Arts class, or the bookstore sells the Monster Book of Monsters, which has to be kept in a cage ('Torn pages were flying everywhere as the books grappled with each other, locked together in furious wrestling matches and snapping aggressively')—the bookseller weeps when someone insists on buying two. And when one boy's wand gets bent, his curses rebound on him; on one noteworthy occasion, he vomits black slugs for several hours.

There are also lovely moments of whimsy and satire. The final exam in the class on Transfiguration is to turn a teapot into a tortoise; afterwards the students compare notes ('Were the tortoises supposed to breathe steam?' 'It still had a willow-patterned shell, d'you think that'll count against me?'). And there is gallows humour: Professor Sprout grows a crop of anthropomorphic [having human characteristics] Mandrakes to chop up and use in a potion to revive certain petrified children; waiting for them to mature so that she can harvest them, she is heartened when they get spots and throw a loud and raucous party. 'The moment they start trying to move into each others' pots,' she tells Harry, 'we'll know they're fully mature.'

A Worthy Addition to the British Fantasy Tradition

Evelyn M. Perry

This article defends *Harry Potter and the Sorcerer's Stone* from its many critics on two fronts, literary and social. *Harry Potter and the Sorcerer's Stone* can be placed in the great English tradition of fantasy novels alongside Lewis Carroll's *Alice in Wonderland* and C.S. Lewis's *Chronicles of Narnia.* J.K. Rowling places her novel in this glorious tradition as Harry must undergo a rite of passage, like the characters in her predecessors' books, through a series of tests. Harry is a classic fantasy hero in the mold of British author T.H. White's young Arthur from *The Once and Future King,* and his rite of passage into young adulthood is in keeping with classic fantasy tradition. Critic Jack Zipes has attacked *Harry Potter* as sexist and stereotypical, but Rowling actually portrays a range of characters in nonstereotypical roles. Admittedly, because *Harry Potter and the Sorcerer's Stone* is set in a magical British boarding school, there are some limitations in the character's economic and social standing. But it must be remembered that *Harry Potter* is a fantasy book, which cannot be expected "to perform the same instructional modeling as contemporary realism" when it comes to issues of race and class. Evelyn M. Perry has taught at Framingham State College in Massachusetts.

Whether because they offer a natural metaphor for coming-of-age audiences transitioning into the adult world, or because—either in cause or effect—they are generally considered most appropriate for the developmental phases and developing psyche of the young adult, the canonized [univer-

Evelyn M. Perry, "Harry Potter and the Sorcerer's Stone," *Beacham's Guide to Literature for Young Adults,* vol. 11, 2001, pp. 214–17. Copyright © 2001 by The Gale Group. Reproduced by permission.

sally accepted] classics of British fantasy traditionally feature young adult protagonists. "The Sword in the Stone," book one of T.H. White's . . . *The Once and Future King* (1965), searches back through history, legend, and the author's own boyhood, to expand the Arthurian legend by contributing the story of Arthur's young adulthood. Appropriately, White, a teacher of young adults, expands Arthurian legend by describing what the young Wart [name of the young King Arthur] learned in his lessons with Merlin in order to explain the genius of Wart's later kingship.

HARRY POTTER IN BRITISH LITERARY TRADITION

But T.H. White is simply one of the more recent authors to artfully and respectfully redefine the traditional parameters of the fantasy genre. He follows such great masters as Lewis Carroll and C.S. Lewis and such beloved characters as Alice Liddell and Lucy Prevensie. In Lewis Carroll's *Alice's Adventures in Wonderland* (1866) and *Through the Looking-Glass* (1872), Carroll describes a series of experiences that mature Alice both emotionally and intellectually in order to prepare her for life as a logical, reasoning, and kind-hearted woman. In the seven books that make up C.S. Lewis's *The Chronicles of Narnia* (1950–1956), Lucy and the Prevensie children (as well as Polly Plumber, Digory Kirke, Eustace Scrubb, and Jill Pole) accomplish a series of moral tasks that underscore Lewis's and the novels' Christian sentiment and earn the characters a place in heaven.

In accordance with, and in honor of, this proud literary history, Rowling's *Harry Potter and the Sorcerer's Stone* begins the story of Harry Potter, age eleven, apprentice wizard and self-doubting hero—a novel that, and a protagonist who, has been inspired by the motifs of classic British fantasy. Clearly, Rowling aspires to further define, and to excel within, the genre of fantasy. In her general examination of the young hero's mentor and his acquisition of wisdom, Rowling's Harry Potter resembles White's young Arthur. Though not privately tutored by Hogwarts headmaster Professor Dumbledore, Harry nevertheless is trained within his school and according to his pedagogic system. And it is at crucial times in the narrative of his training that Harry is given the opportunity to consult with Dumbledore: when he develops a dangerous preoccupation with the Mirror of Erised, when he must negotiate the prudent use of the invisibility cloak, and after he has successfully (and for the second time) defeated "He Who Shall Not Be Named." Additionally, Dumbledore resembles Merlin both personally and physically; he is an avid lover of books and wisdom who wears flowing robes and a long, white beard. This resemblance suggests not only how much White's master wizard has influenced—and continues to influence—audience expectation, but how that influence has determined Rowling's use of classic fantasy motifs.

HARRY'S RITES OF PASSAGE

Rowling also credits Lewis Carroll and C.S. Lewis through her description, and use, of a reflective device and a train ride to achieve passage into a fantastic other-world. In a manner that suggests a parallel to the rites of passage of young adulthood, Harry Potter boards a train at platform nine and three quarters at King's Cross station. Harry's trip will bring him to the wondrously magical and separate (though whimsically and pointedly parallel) world of Hogwarts School of Witchcraft and Wizardry. After many railway trips, many happy adventures, and the conclusive suggestion that they might be outgrowing such adventures, the Prevensie children of Lewis's *The Chronicles of Narnia* access the kingdom of heaven when they are killed in a train wreck. In Carroll's *Through the Looking-Glass,* Alice speeds through the countryside of her own parallel world, the reversed world of "nonsense" on the other side of a mirror, while she is engaged in a giant game of chess that she must win in order to return transformed and victorious to the "real," that is adult, world. Harry passes the preparatory "test" of the Mirror of Erised (with a great deal of help and guidance from Professor Dumbledore), gaining the strength and confidence necessary to help him (along with Ron Weasley) face the challenge of the giant chess game towards the end of *Harry Potter and the Sorcerer's Stone*. Alice's success in the chess game, involving the maturity required to eschew the paradoxes (bureaucracy) of the Red Queen and her supporters (political, governmental systems), informs Rowling's description of Harry's and Ron's actions during the giant chess game, as well as our perceptions of them. Chess, a game of logic requiring patience and experience, tests and proves both the capabilities of reason and fantasy, and Harry and his friends must further establish themselves as heroes by exercising both of these capabilities—much in the way the audience does in the act of reading, in the act of entering a reflective art form.

Thus, as a fellow reader and creating author, in book one of the Harry Potter series, *Harry Potter and the Sorcerer's Stone,* Rowling gives due credit to the precedents of her literary forebears and extends a hand to those writers who may hope to follow. And the readers and keepers of the tradition of classic, British fantasy, would do well to acknowledge agreement in Rowling's debt as well as the reader's debt to Rowling.

HARRY POTTER CRITICIZED

In a television interview aired in July of 2000—just prior to the release of the much-anticipated fourth Harry Potter book—eminent children's and young adult literature critic and scholar Jack Zipes described Rowling's fiction as formulaic and sexist. Because Zipes was not given the chance to fully support his thesis within the format of the televised sound bite, any response to his thesis must be based, in part, on conjecture. Nevertheless, that Rowling's Harry Potter books should be described as formulaic is problematic. The Harry Potter books are, after all, a series, and, at least thus far, the action takes place during the academic year. Aside from some scattered highlights of Harry's summer holidays, the plot of *Harry Potter and the Sorcerer's Stone* follows the unchanging rhythm of a highly structured educational calendar. While an academic year provides a useful template by which Rowling may structure her fiction, the description of such a template as formulaic seems unfair and a refusal to acknowledge just how reliant a young adult audience is on the academic calendar—or how useful it is to the plot structure of British fantasy. Indeed, Lewis Carroll's Alice has her adventures while she is not engaged with her studies in both *Alice's Adventures in Wonderland* and *Through the Looking-Glass,* and throughout C.S. Lewis's *The Narnia Chronicles,* his young protagonists travel to and from Narnia while on vacation from school.

Defending Harry Potter

In terms of Rowling's potential sexism, it may be likewise argued that, as she follows and departs from a traditional academic structure in her novels, so too does Rowling follow and depart from traditional gender roles. Mrs. Dursley characterizes the standard housewife in the opening pages of *Harry Potter and the Sorcerer's Stone,* while Mr. Dursley presents us with a mock-image of the bowler-capped British businessman. But it should be noted that Mrs. and Mr. Dursley are not beloved characters (certainly not characters after whom young readers would be inclined to model themselves), and that other characters do not always line up according to standard expectations of gender: Professor McGonagall is a witch and a teacher to be respected and admired, Madame Hooch coaches the (co-ed) Quidditch team, Hermione Granger is as capable of getting herself out (or in) trouble as Ron Weasley or Harry himself; Professor Dumbledore is a homebody, Professor Quirrell is a weak and fearful wizard, and Hagrid has undeniably strong mothering instincts. Ultimately, that some of Rowling's characters inhabit traditional gender roles while others do not may be the best, and most elegant, argument against the enforcement of those roles.

CONCERNS ABOUT STEREOTYPES

And yet, the defense of Rowling's fiction as formulaic or sexist does raise some interesting considerations regarding social concerns in *Harry Potter and the Sorcerer's Stone.* Because the novel follows the British school year, there are few—if any—references to non-Christian faiths and practices. Thus, the witches and wizards at Hogwarts celebrate Christmas—even despite their supposedly pagan history. Harry is able to afford Hogwarts because of the large inheritance left to him by his parents, a detail that can serve to example a limited representation of economic stratification. Due to his last name and his red hair, we might assume that Ron Weasley is of Irish descent; such an assumption would then lead us to argue that the depiction of Ron's family, poor and well-populated, reveals a prejudice against Irish Catholics in Rowling, Great Britain, or both. Similarly, while several referenced characters represent other races and ethnicities (Lee Jordan, for example, is black), the main protagonists of the novel, the characters in whom readers are most invested, are white.

A WORTHY BOOK OF FANTASY

Considering the anxiety that contemporary audiences and critics have regarding the fair and equal representation of peoples in literature—and particularly in literature for children and young adults—these observations are both legitimate and unavoidable. But, too, readers must consider the transcendent possibilities of fantasy novels. If one of the benefits of fantasy is to remove the reader from an oppressive social reality, and thereby to offer a lens through which he or she might critique and resolve social injustices, critics cannot expect fantasy to perform the same instructional modeling as contemporary realism. This is not an excuse or a justification, and it is not because fantasy does not mirror and model life as does all literature (and all art). It is because, as a genre, fantasy behaves according to its own history, tradition, and purpose. Though it is appropriate to expect contemporary fantasy to fairly and accurately represent social diversity, a more appropriate concern for fantasy may be how well it models the readers' ability to see themselves within their social system and how convincingly it argues for their deserved equality. That Rowling's *Harry Potter and the Sorcerer's Stone* does, indeed, reflect and address social diversity, and that *Harry Potter and the Sorcerer's Stone* inspires both young and old readers to see their worlds in new and different ways (ways that may result in social activism and change), offers a strong argument for our acknowledgment of *Harry Potter and the Sorcerer's Stone* as fantastic literature worthy of a place in the canon.

CHAPTER 3

Critical Response to *Harry Potter*

READINGS ON
J.K. ROWLING

Harry Potter and the Sorcerer's Stone Is a Classic

Charles Taylor

In this review of *Harry Potter and the Sorcerer's Stone*, Charles Taylor suggests that the reader soon gets the feeling that J.K. Rowling's first novel is a classic. *Harry Potter and the Sorcerer's Stone* rises above ordinary children's fiction through the realism of its fantastical plot and through the cleverness of the characterizations. Taylor cites what he believes is Rowling's most clever invention, the mirror that reflects a person's fondest desires. There is a beauty in the passage describing Harry's confrontation with the mirror that forces one to admire the craft of the novelist. The novel itself is wonderful, and it need not impart to the reader any "lesson" to be considered a classic, not only for children but for adults as well. Charles Taylor has been a contributing writer to *Salon*, an online magazine.

The hero of J.K. Rowling's "Harry Potter and the Sorcerer's Stone" is an outsider, one who, like many other outsiders in kids' literature, learns to value the things that have always made him feel separate from the people around him, and who also learns that the means of escape from his solitary existence has been within him all along. The book is a dream of belonging, and of discovering self-sufficiency and courage. What matters, though, is the flesh Rowling puts on those thematic bones. I don't think you can read 100 pages of "Harry Potter and the Sorcerer's Stone" before you start feeling that unmistakable shiver that tells you you're reading a classic. Rowling's own story is irresistible: a single mom, she began writing the book while unemployed and got a grant from the Scottish Arts Council enabling her to finish it. The first book in a cycle of seven, "Harry Potter" has become something of a children's publishing phenomenon, one of those rare books that crosses over to adult readers.

HARRY AS A YOUNG HERO

Harry Potter's life starts with one of the tragedies that heroes carry with them like scars (in fact, he bears a mysterious lightning-shaped scar on his forehead). Harry's parents are killed when he is just an infant, and he grows up in the shabby care of his aunt and uncle, Vernon and Petunia Dursley, and their horror of a son, Dudley. The Dursleys are the sort of oppressively ordinary dullards that [children's writer Roald] Dahl took delight in savaging—not *because* they're ordinary, but because they're so utterly self-satisfied about being ordinary, and so suspicious of anyone who isn't. They're characters who epitomize the word the book's wizards use to describe people without magical powers: Muggles. (We've all got a few Muggles in our families.) Within the stultified suburban London confines of 4 Privet Drive, Harry lives a Grimm [a pun on fairy tale writers, the Brothers Grimm] existence, sleeping in a cupboard under the stairs (which he shares with spiders) and being the whipping boy for Dudley and his sluggard pals. Life continues this way until Harry is 11, when suddenly an emissary from Hogwarts, a school that has trained generations of wizards, drops into his life. The messenger, an enormous bear of a man named Hagrid (who will become Harry's protector), informs Harry that he is in fact the son of wizards killed by the dark wizard Voldemort. Voldemort was not able to kill Harry (he could inflict no more damage than that lightning-shaped scar), though the word is that the dark wizard is biding his time, consolidating his power. With his own training ahead of him, Harry is whisked away to Hogwarts and there begin his adventures.

Rowling is the most matter-of-fact fantasy writer you

could hope for. Each marvel—like the owls who deliver morning mail at Hogwarts, or the school sport of Quidditch, a kind of field hockey played in the air while riding broomsticks—is treated in a one-thing-after-another manner that keeps any hint of preciousness from creeping in. Her straightforwardness (with just the right degree of the nasty humor kids love) keeps her writing grounded. She's come up with a nifty metaphor for the way in which magic exists in the guise of the ordinary: The world of wizards exists in comfortable parallel to the Muggle world, visible only to those with powers, happily invisible to everyone else. Thus, the train to Hogwarts leaves from a hidden platform at King's Cross, and the wizard business district is accessible only from a walled courtyard behind a pub.

CHARACTERS WHO LIVE UP TO THEIR NAMES

"Harry Potter and the Sorcerer's Stone" unites the English novel of school day exploits with the humorous, macabre fantasy that Dahl perfected. In the time-honored tradition of the latter, Harry quickly locates a best friend (Ron Weasley, the latest in a long line of siblings who've attended Hogwarts, his being the sort of middle-class family that sacrifices to send the kids to a good school), a nemesis (the snobby rich kid Draco Malfoy), the class overachiever who nonetheless becomes his friend (Hermione Granger), the little kid made to be picked on (Neville Longbottom) and the teacher who seems to have it out for him (Snape). It's the best compliment I can pay Rowling that she's created characters who live up to the names she's picked out for them. They're types, yes, but so fully drawn that they break the molds.

MORE THAN JUST AN AMUSING BOOK

I realize that the book I'm describing sounds like no more than an amusing diversion. But . . . literature is a diversion that offers a way back to life. And while comfort may be one of the goals of those children's books that are fantasies of belonging, there's nothing cushy or insular about the best children's books, which never deny the possibility of pain or loss. You might even argue that the tragedies of these books hurt even more (the way the tragedies of great musicals do) because they occur within an idealized fantasy world. "Harry Potter" reassures its readers that they won't get lost as they enter into new experiences, but at the same time it never denies the ache of what you leave behind. That's the emotional balance Rowling maintains, and I can sum up the keenness of this book's emotions by quoting the passage that describes the author's most remarkable and moving invention. Prowling around the school one night after lights out, Harry stumbles upon a room that contains a mirror. Looking in it, he's startled to see himself surrounded by a crowd of people with eyes and hair just like him. Harry doesn't know that the mirror shows whoever looks into it their heart's fondest desire, but the realization dawns on him that he is "looking at his family, for the first time in his life." Rowling continues:

> The Potters smiled and waved at Harry and he stared hungrily back at them, his hands pressed flat against the glass as though he was hoping to fall right through it and reach them. He had a powerful kind of ache inside him, half joy, half terrible sadness.

> How long he stood there, he didn't know. The reflections did not fade and he looked and looked until a distant noise brought him back to his senses. He couldn't stay here, he had to find a way back to bed. He tore his eyes away from his mother's face, whispered, "I'll come back," and hurried from the room.

The beauty of that passage, in both conception and execution (Rowling is an astonishingly visual writer), needs no explication. But perhaps you have to have made your way through too many exquisitely crafted novels that didn't make you feel anything beyond a vague admiration for their craft to understand why reading a passage like that can seem as necessary as coming upon a drink of cool water when you're parched. So I don't want to condescend to J.K. Rowling by saying she's written a wonderful children's novel. She's written a wonderful novel, period. And to those who insist that novels should impart lessons, let the lesson of "Harry Potter" be the only distinction worth making in literature: separating the Muggles from the wizards.

The *Harry Potter* Books Are Not Classics

Harold Bloom

This essay, which originally appeared in the editorial pages of the *Wall Street Journal,* is perhaps the most well known attack on the *Harry Potter* books. Its author, the brilliant Yale University and New York University professor Harold Bloom, admits to having read only the first book in the series. Yet he finds *Harry Potter and the Sorcerer's Stone* to be a poorly written, cliché-ridden, unimaginative non-classic that will not stand the test of time. "Can 35 million book buyers be wrong?" he asks, and answers, without hesitation, "Yes." Bloom sees the *Harry Potter* phenomenon as part of a larger picture of indiscriminate reading in our culture, where the greatest books are ignored and lesser works are promoted. There are many books, like *Harry Potter,* he argues, that undeservingly get thrust into the mainstream of popular culture by a public that does not really understand how or why to read a book. Harold Bloom's many books include *Shakespeare: The Invention of the Human, The Western Canon, The Book of J,* and *Stories and Poems for Extremely Intelligent Children of All Ages.*

Taking arms against Harry Potter, at this moment, is to emulate Hamlet taking arms against a sea of troubles. By opposing the sea, you won't end it. The Harry Potter epiphenomenon will go on, doubtless for some time, as J.R.R. Tolkien [author of *Lord of the Rings*] did and then wane.

The official newspaper of our dominant counter-culture, The New York Times, has been startled by the Potter books into establishing a new policy for its not very literate book review. Rather than crowd out the [John] Grishams, [Tom] Clancys, [Michael] Crichtons, [Stephen] Kings and other vastly popular prose fictions on its fiction bestseller list, the Potter volumes will now lead a separate children's list. J.K. Rowling, the chronicler of Harry Potter, thus has an unusual distinction: She has changed the policy of the policy-maker.

HARRY POTTER LACKS IMAGINATIVE VISION

I read new children's literature, when I can find some of any value, but had not tried Rowling until now. I have just concluded the 300 pages of the first book in the series. "Harry Potter and the Sorcerer's Stone," purportedly the best of the lot. Though the book is not well written, that is not in itself a crucial liability. It is much better to see the movie, "The Wizard of Oz," than to read the book upon which it was based, but even the book possessed an authentic imaginative vision. "Harry Potter and the Sorcerer's Stone" does not, so that one needs to look elsewhere for the book's (and its sequels') remarkable success. Such speculation should follow an account of how and why Harry Potter asks to be read.

The ultimate model for Harry Potter is "Tom Brown's School Days" by Thomas Hughes, published in 1857. The book depicts the Rugby School presided over by the formidable Thomas Arnold, remembered now primarily as the father of Matthew Arnold, the Victorian critic-poet. But Hughes's book, still quite readable, was realism, not fantasy. Rowling has taken "Tom Brown's School Days" and re-seen it in the magical mirror of Tolkien. The resultant blend of a schoolboy ethos with a liberation from the constraints of reality-testing may read oddly to me, but is exactly what millions of children and their parents desire and welcome at this time.

In what follows, I may at times indicate some of the inadequacies of "Harry Potter." But I will keep in mind that a host are reading it who simply will not read superior fare, such as Kenneth Grahame's "The Wind in the Willows" or the "Alice" books of Lewis Carroll. Is it better that they read Rowling than not read at all? Will they advance from Rowling to more difficult pleasures?

THE PLOT OF "HARRY POTTER AND THE SORCERER'S STONE"

Rowling presents two Englands, mundane and magical, divided not by social classes, but by the distinction between the "perfectly normal" (mean and selfish) and the adherents of sorcery. The sorcerers indeed seem as middle-class as the Muggles, the name the witches and wizards give to the common sort, since those addicted to magic send their sons and daughters off to Hogwarts, a Rugby School where only witchcraft and wizardry are taught. Hogwarts is presided over by Albus Dumbledore as Headmaster, he being Rowling's version of Tolkien's Gandalf [a powerful wizard]. The young future sorcerers are just like any other budding Britons, only more so, sports and food being primary preoccupations.

Harry Potter, now the hero of so many millions of children and adults, is raised by dreadful Muggle relatives after his sorcerer parents are murdered by the wicked Voldemort, a wizard gone trollish and, finally, post-human. Precisely why poor Harry is handed over by the sorcerer elders to his piggish aunt and uncle is never clarified by Rowling, but it is a nice touch, suggesting again how conventional the alternative Britain truly is. They consign their potential hero-wizard to his nasty blood-kin, rather than let him be reared by amiable warlocks and witches, who would know him for one of their own.

The child Harry thus suffers the hateful ill treatment of the Dursleys, Muggles of the most Muggleworthy sort, and of their sadistic son, his cousin Dudley. For some early pages we might be in Ken Russell's film of "Tommy," the rock-opera by The Who, except that the prematurely wise Harry is much healthier than Tommy. A born survivor, Harry holds on until the sorcerers rescue him and send him off to Hogwarts, to enter upon the glory of his schooldays.

Hogwarts enchants many of Harry's fans, perhaps because it is much livelier than the schools they attend, but it seems to me an academy more tiresome than grotesque. When the future witches and wizards of Great Britain are not studying how to cast a spell, they preoccupy themselves with bizarre intramural sports. It is rather a relief when Harry heroically suffers the ordeal of a confrontation with Voldemort, which the youth handles admirably.

HARRY POTTER IS NOT A CLASSIC

One can reasonably doubt that "Harry Potter and the Sorcerer's Stone" is going to prove a classic of children's literature, but Rowling, whatever the aesthetic weakness of her work, is at least a millennial index to our popular culture. So huge an audience gives her importance akin to rock stars, movie idols, TV anchors, and successful politicians. Her prose style, heavy on cliché, makes no demands upon her readers. In an arbitrarily chosen single page—page 4—of the first Harry Potter book, I count seven clichés, all of the "stretch his legs" variety.

How to read "Harry Potter and the Sorcerer's Stone"? Why, very quickly, to begin with, perhaps also to make an end. Why read it? Presumably, if you cannot be persuaded to read anything better, Rowling will have to do. Is there any redeeming educational use to Rowling? Is there any to Stephen King? Why read, if what you read will not enrich mind or spirit or personality? For all I know, the actual wizards and witches of Britain, or of America, may provide an alternative culture for more people than is commonly realized.

Perhaps Rowling appeals to millions of reader non-readers because they sense her wistful sincerity, and want to join her world, imaginary or not. She feeds a vast hunger for unreality; can that be bad? At least her fans are momentarily emancipated from their screens, and so may not forget wholly the sensation of turning the pages of a book, any book.

And yet I feel a discomfort with the Harry Potter mania,

and I hope that my discontent is not merely a highbrow snobbery, or a nostalgia for a more literate fantasy to beguile (shall we say) intelligent children of all ages. Can more than 35 million book buyers, and their offspring, be wrong? Yes, they have been, and will continue to be so for as long as they persevere with Potter.

A vast concourse of inadequate works, for adults and for children, crams the dustbins of the ages. At a time when public judgment is no better and no worse than what is proclaimed by the ideological cheerleaders who have so destroyed humanistic study, anything goes. The cultural critics will, soon enough, introduce Harry Potter into their college curriculum, and The New York Times will go on celebrating another confirmation of the dumbing down it leads and exemplifies.

Harry Potter Is Unsuitable for Children

Richard Abanes

In this excerpt from his book, *Harry Potter and the Bible: The Menace Behind the Magick*, Richard Abanes contends that J.K. Rowling's books are inappropriate for children. Rowling herself has stated, Abanes says, that the books were not originally intended for children. He suggests therefore, that the gruesome and violent imagery and scenes in *Harry Potter* are highly disturbing and that Rowling's humor is often cruel. These values are inconsistent with messages that adults should be sharing with children. Abanes quotes specific biblical passages to show how messages in *Harry Potter* are out of sync with Christian values and concludes that the *Harry Potter* books are harmful to children. Richard Abanes is a self-described evangelical Christian and an authority on cults and worldwide religions. He is author of numerous books, including *One Nation Under Gods: A History of the Mormon Church, End-Time Visions: The Road to Armageddon?* and *Cults, New Religious Movements, and Your Family: A Guide to Ten Non-Christian Groups Seeking to Convert Your Loved Ones.*

During a National Public Radio interview with Diane Rehm, J.K. Rowling explained that she did not necessarily write her books for children. She actually penned them as novels that she herself, as an adult, would enjoy reading. Rowling also mentioned that she kept in mind the kind of book she might have wanted to read as a little girl. Interestingly, Rowling has stated: "When I was quite young, my parents never said books were off limits. . . . As a child, I read a lot of adult books. I

Richard Abanes, *Harry Potter and the Bible: The Menace Behind the Magick*. Camp Hill, PA: Horizon, 2001. Copyright © 2001 by Horizon Books, a division of Christian Publications, Inc. Reproduced by permission.

don't think you should censor kids' reading material. It's important just to let them go do what they need to do."

Rowling apparently feels that adult-oriented material is perfectly suitable for children, which may explain why forty-three percent of her books sold in 1999 were to readers older than fourteen. And according to the N.D. Group, a leading market research firm that tracks book-buying in 12,000 households, nearly thirty percent of Harry Potter purchases were made for readers thirty-five or older. Some adult readers are so captivated by Harry that they have begun concocting their own "fan-written" Potter adult stories.

For example, there is "Harry Potter and the Paradigm of Uncertainty," which can be found on the Internet at e-Groups. Lori Summers, author of this narrative in progress, describes it as a PG-13 story for adult fans of the Harry Potter series. It takes place twelve years in the future, is extremely romantic in nature, and puts Harry living in one big dorm with several other witches (females) and wizards (males). Summers stresses it is not for children.

HARRY POTTER CONTAINS MATERIAL INAPPROPRIATE FOR CHILDREN

But adult Harry Potter fans need not scan the Internet for "mature" material, especially when it comes to scenes involving gratuitous violence, gruesome images, cruelty and humor that often borders on perversity. One of the most grisly characters to come from Rowling is a ghost named "Nearly Headless Nick" who lived 500 years earlier and died on a Halloween night by being struck on the neck forty-five times with a blunt ax. He first appears in Chapter 7 of Book I:

> "I know who you are!" said Ron suddenly. "My brothers told me about you—you're Nearly Headless Nick!"
>
> . . . "Nearly Headless?" [asked Seamus Finnigan]. "How can you be nearly headless?"
>
> "Like *this*," he said irritably. He seized his left ear and pulled.

His whole head swung off his neck and fell onto his shoulder as if it was on a hinge. Someone had obviously tried to behead him, but not done it properly.

Then, in Chapter 15, readers are treated to a horrible scene featuring Professor Quirrell, who is possessed by Voldemort:

[O]ut of the shadows, a hooded figure came crawling across the ground like some stalking beast. . . . The cloaked figure reached the unicorn, lowered its head over the wound in the animal's side, and began to drink its blood.

Scenes less gory, but equally disturbing, are those wherein cruelty/vengeance are presented as acceptable. Hagrid, for instance, performs an illegal spell against Harry's cousin, Dudley. (He gives Dudley an extremely painful pig's tail that has to be surgically removed.) This is not done because Dudley himself acts improperly toward Hagrid. It is done to punish Mr. Dursley for insulting Dumbledore. Rather than attacking Mr. Dursley, Hagrid turns his revenge against Dudley (an innocent individual) as a way of more gravely hurting the father.

Revenge also appears in a Diagon Alley scene, where Harry finds *Curses and Countercurses (Bewitch Your Friends and Befuddle Your Enemies with the Latest Revenges: Hair Loss, Jelly Legs, Tongue-Tying and Much, Much More)* by Professor Vindictus Viridian. When Hagrid drags Harry away so they can stay on their time schedule, Harry says: "I was trying to find out how to curse Dudley." Instead of correcting Harry and pointing him in a better direction, Hagrid replies: "I'm not sayin' that's not a good idea, but yer not ter use magic in the Muggle world except in very special circumstances."

HARRY POTTER DOES NOT PROMOTE CHRISTIAN VALUES

A display of similar attitudes by other "good" characters throughout the Potter series creates a running theme that is not difficult to discern: It is appropriate to return evil for evil, and treat others well only if they treat you well. As Rowling herself has stated about her main character: "Harry wants to get back at Dudley. . . . [A]nd we readers want him to get back at Dudley. And, in the long run, trust me, he will." Contrast this approach with what Scripture says regarding enemies and our treatment of them:

- Thou shalt not avenge. . . . [L]ove thy neighbour as thyself. (Leviticus 19:18)
- Recompense to no man evil for evil. . . . If it be possible, as much as lieth in you, live peaceably with all men. . . . Be not overcome of evil, but overcome evil with good. (Romans 12:17–18, 21)
- Love your enemies, do good to them which hate you, bless them that curse you, and pray for them which despitefully use you. (Luke 6:27–28)

In yet another scene, Professor Snape—the disliked potions teacher—is seen limping due to some sort of injury to his leg. Harry wonders what is wrong with Snape, and Ron bitterly replies: "Dunno, but I hope it's really hurting him." Again, the Bible reads very differently: "Rejoice not when thine enemy falleth, and let not thine heart be glad when he stumbleth" (Proverbs 24:17).

Clearly, Rowling's books include a great deal of material that is inappropriate for children as well as inconsistent with Christian values.

Despite these flaws, Book I has become a best-seller around the world. According to an ABCnews.com report, it is because Rowling's books "show the complexities of children, and the ambiguities of childhood—the delights and fears of separation and exploration." But as we have seen, these volumes also contain material that is both unsuitable and harmful to children.

Harry Potter Must Not Be Banned

Judy Blume

In this essay, Judy Blume uses irony and humor to attack those groups who seek to ban books for illogical reasons. A well-known writer of young-adult fiction herself, Blume fears that any group of naysayers with a grudge against a particular book can now effectively have the book banned from schools and libraries. Blume knows about book banning from an intimate perspective, because her own stories have been attacked for being too realistic. That is, they do not attempt to hide the unpleasant side of life. J.K. Rowling's books, on the other hand, are subject to attack for the completely opposite reason: They are too fantastic and their portrait of wizards and witches is objectionable to some groups. But Blume feels that the *Harry Potter* series, like L. Frank Baum's *Oz* series before it, is simply a wonderful reading experience. And that should be enough to keep *Harry Potter* on bookshelves everywhere. Judy Blume is the author of over twenty novels, including *Forever. . .* and *Are You There God? It's Me, Margaret.*

I happened to be in London . . . on the very day "Harry Potter and the Prisoner of Azkaban," the third book in the wildly popular series by J.K. Rowling, was published. I couldn't believe my good fortune. I rushed to the bookstore to buy a copy, knowing this simple act would put me up there with the best grandmas in the world. The book was still months away from publication in the United States, and I have an 8-year-old grandson who is a big Harry Potter fan.

It's a good thing when children enjoy books, isn't it? Most of us think so. But like many children's books these days, the Harry Potter series has recently come under fire. In Minnesota, Michigan, New York, California and South Carolina, parents who feel the books promote interest in the occult [matters involving the supernatural] have called for their removal from classrooms and school libraries.

I knew this was coming. The only surprise is that it took so long—as long as it took for the zealots who claim they're protecting children from evil (and evil can be found lurking everywhere these days) to discover that children actually like these books. If children are excited about a book, it must be suspect.

BANNING HARRY POTTER

I'm not exactly unfamiliar with this line of thinking, having had various books of mine banned from schools over the last 20 years. In my books, it's reality that's seen as corrupting. With Harry Potter, the perceived danger is fantasy. After all, Harry and his classmates attend the celebrated Hogwarts School of Witchcraft and Wizardry. According to certain adults, these stories teach witchcraft, sorcery and satanism. But hey, if it's not one "ism," it's another. I mean Madeleine L'Engle's "A Wrinkle in Time" has been targeted by censors for promoting New Ageism [a late twentieth-century social movement drawing on ancient concepts] and Mark Twain's "Adventures of Huckleberry Finn" for promoting racism. Gee, where does that leave the kids?

The real danger is not in the books, but in laughing off those who would ban them. The protests against Harry Potter follow a tradition that has been growing since the early 1980's and often leaves school principals trembling with fear that is then passed down to teachers and librarians.

What began with the religious right has spread to the politically correct. (Remember the uproar in Brooklyn in 1998 when a teacher was criticized for reading a book entitled

"Nappy Hair" [a supposed slur against African Americans] to her class?) And now the gate is open so wide that some parents believe they have the right to demand immediate removal of any book for any reason from school or classroom libraries. The list of gifted teachers and librarians who find their jobs in jeopardy for defending their students' right to read, to imagine, to question, grows every year.

BANNING BOOKS DOESN'T MAKE SENSE

My grandson was bewildered when I tried to explain why some adults don't want their children reading about Harry Potter. "But that doesn't make any sense!" he said. J.K. Rowling is on a book tour in America right now. She's probably befuddled by the brouhaha, too. After all, she was just trying to tell a good story.

My husband and I like to reminisce about how, when we were 9, we read straight through L. Frank Baum's Oz series [including *The Wizard of Oz*], books filled with wizards and witches. And you know what those subversive tales taught us? That we loved to read! In those days I used to dream of flying. I may have been small and powerless in real life, but in my imagination I was able to soar.

At the rate we're going, I can imagine next year's headline: "'Goodnight Moon' [a well-known book for very young children] Banned for Encouraging Children to Communicate With Furniture." And we all know where that can lead, don't we?

Harry Potter Is Just for Children

William Safire

William Safire's column on *Harry Potter* derives from the awarding of a literary prize to Irish poet Seamus Heaney instead of to J.K. Rowling for *Harry Potter*. Safire wholeheartedly agrees with the selection. In Safire's opinion, all of the hype about Harry Potter should not disguise the fact that Rowling's books are for children. They do not rise above this designation to exist on two levels (for adults as well as children) as do some great children's books such as Mark Twain's *Huck Finn* and Lewis Carroll's *Alice in Wonderland*. There is nothing wrong with the *Potter* books being for children, Safire suggests. But adults should not mistake them for classic literature. Safire bases this opinion on the reading of a single *Potter* novel, *Harry Potter and the Sorcerer's Stone*. But he is adamant in his belief that despite their success on the best-seller list, J.K. Rowling's series holds in it nothing deep enough for serious adult reading. William Safire was a White House adviser and speechwriter during the Nixon years. He has served as a member of the *New York Times* editorial staff, and he won a Pulitzer Prize for distinguished commentary in 1978.

With the help of a tall blond model from Texas, the British have just upheld the side of adult culture in the English-speaking world.

They resisted the pressure to award a top literary prize to J.K. Rowling for her superselling series of Harry Potter books. Instead, the top honor again went to the Irish poet

Seamus Heaney, this time for his translation of the Anglo-Saxon epic "Beowulf."

PUTTING POTTER IN PERSPECTIVE

That was a relief. With the orphan wizard dominating best-seller lists, the Harry Potter phenomenon needs a little perspective.

These are children's books. Their glory is that their hero's magical charm has captivated a world of kids, inculcating the reading habit in pre-teens who otherwise would be seduced into interactive games of mayhem. Getting children to read is no small blessing, and Rowling has provided them with a key to literacy.

These are not, however, books for adults. Unlike [Mark Twain's] "Huckleberry Finn" or [Lewis Carroll's] "Alice in Wonderland," the Potter series is not written on two levels, entertaining one generation while instructing another. Rather, it is in the category of Tom Swift [book series about a boy inventor published under the pen name Victor Appleton] and [Hugh Lofting's] Dr. Dolittle; I was hooked on reading by them, but have laid aside my electric rifle [that Tom Swift uses] and no longer talk to horses [as does Dr. Dolittle].

The trouble is not that children are being lured into belief in witchcraft, as some tut-tutting clerics complain; Western civilization has survived Merlin's magic in the tales of King Arthur. Nor will poor children be corrupted by tales of life in upper-middle-class English boarding schools.

The trouble is that grown-ups are buying these books ostensibly to read to kids, but actually to read for themselves. As Philip Hensher warns in the *Independent* newspaper, this leads to "the infantilization [reduction of adult to children] of adult culture, the loss of a sense of what a classic really is."

Scholarly tomes will be written about the underlying motifs of the Potter series, justifying its adult readership. Steven Spielberg [film director who backed out of the Harry Potter project] will slip a little social significance into his movie treatment, further furrowing academic brows. But this is not just dumbing down; it is growing down. The purpose of reading, once you get the hang of it, is not merely to follow the action of a plot, but to learn about characters, explore different ideas and enter other minds.

"Huckleberry Finn" is a classic because it used the device of a boy's coming of age to illuminate a nation's painful transformation. When Lewis Carroll took us through the looking glass, he dealt with madness and injustice in this world by mocking a parallel world. Critics delight in annotating the allusions in such books.

WHY HARRY POTTER LOST THE AWARD

Not in "Harry Potter and the Sorcerer's Stone." That's the one I read, noting its nice deployment of the standard tricks. I also enjoy short films, featuring anthropomorphic [human-like] porcine cartoon characters [Porky pig], that end with "Th-th-th-that's all, folks!" But prizeworthy culture it ain't; more than a little is a waste of adult time.

That's why my hat is off to Jerry Hall, the intelligent Texan and mother of four, divorced from [Rolling Stones lead singer] Mick Jagger, who still sort of lives with her. She is reported to have cast the swing vote on the judging panel for Seamus Heaney. That Nobel laureate accepted the $35,000 prize with a line from "Beowulf," "Fate go ever, as fate must" (a somewhat fatalistic response). The *Guardian* [English newspaper] headline: "Heaney pips Harry Potter."

It's about time Potter was pipped (narrowly defeated). His creator, Ms. Rowling, deserved the lesser award she received for best children's book. But let us not exalt Potter, either, as a cultural icon. Adults make a part of their lives only the works that have meaning.

Remember Dorothy in her transforming ruby slippers in *The Wizard of Oz*? Frank Baum's book, cemented into our culture by the 1939 Victor Fleming movie starring [American actress] Judy Garland, was a children's fantasy, complete with a Wicked Witch of the West, but dealt deftly with heartlessness, mindlessness and cowardice.

Its symbols became part of our culture. Munchkins presume to advise candidates following the yellow brick road to power, and behind the curtain we discover that the fearsome wizard of bombast is only a frightened Frank Morgan [the actor who plays the wizard]. For adults, Harry Potter may reign over the best-seller lists, but he has yet to heave his philosopher's stone over the rainbow.

Harry Potter Upholds the Wonder of Childhood

Alison Lurie

In this review of the first three *Harry Potter* books, novelist
Alison Lurie places J.K. Rowling's stories in the Anglo-
American tradition of childhood tales. Childhood is not
looked on as being exceptional in other cultures, but since
the Romantic era of the late 1700s, English and American
authors have treated youth as a special time in one's life, a
time when innocence and joy can be fully expressed. This
philosophy is the reason, she suggests, why there are so
many great English children's tales, *Harry Potter* among
them. As in the fantasy novels of great English authors
J.R.R. Tolkien (*The Hobbit* and *The Lord of the Rings*) and
C.S. Lewis (the *Narnia* series), the *Harry Potter* books portray a classic struggle of good and evil. J.K. Rowling's own
journey from rags to riches is another classic tale in literary
tradition that is almost as interesting as the books themselves. Alison Lurie has taught at Cornell University. She is
the Pulitzer Prize–winning author of *Foreign Affairs* and
numerous other novels. Like J.K. Rowling, she has written
a book about whimsical animals entitled *Fabulous Beasts*,
and she has also delved into the area of children's books
with *Don't Tell the Grown-Ups: The Subversive Power of
Children's Literature.*

Why are so many of the best-known children's books British
or American? Other countries have produced a single brilliant
classic or series: Denmark, for instance, has Andersen's fairy
tales, Italy has *Pinocchio*, France has *Babar*, Finland has
Moomintroll. A list of famous children's books in English,

however, could easily take up the rest of this column.

One explanation may be that in Britain and America more people never quite grow up. They may sometimes put on a good show of maturity, but secretly they remain children, longing for the pleasures and privileges of childhood that once were, or were said to be, theirs. And there are some reasons for them to do so.

CHILDHOOD IS SPECIAL IN ENGLISH-SPEAKING NATIONS

In most nations there is nothing especially wonderful about being a child of school age. For the first four or five years boys and girls may be petted and indulged, but after that they are usually expected to become little adults as soon as possible: responsible, serious, future-oriented. But in English-speaking nations, ever since the late eighteenth century, poets and philosophers and educators have maintained that there is something wonderful and unique about childhood: that simply to be young is to be naturally good and great. It may be no coincidence that the romantic glorification of youth of the Sixties and early Seventies was most evident in America and Britain, or that when they want to make an especially touching appeal to voters, American politicians always speak of "our kids."

Because childhood is seen as a superior condition, many Americans and Britons are naturally reluctant to give it up. They tend to think of themselves as young much longer, and cling to childhood attitudes and amusements. On vacation, and in the privacy of their homes, they readily revert to an earlier age: they wear childish clothes and play childish games and sometimes read children's books.

The authors of great juvenile fiction, whatever their nationality, often continue to think and feel as children. They are spontaneous, dreamy, imaginative, unpredictable. E. Nesbit spent many hours building a toy town out of blocks and kitchenware, and wrote a book, *The Magic City*, about it; Laurent deBrunhoff, who has continued his father's *Babar* series for many years and is now over seventy, still climbs trees with childish skill and delight. James Barrie spent his summer holidays playing pirates and Indians with the four Davies boys, and Lewis Carroll also much preferred the company of children to that of adults.

Since so many juvenile classics are written by people like this, it should be no surprise that they often take the side of children against adults. These books are, in the deepest sense, subversive. They make fun of grown-ups and expose adult pretensions and failings; they suggest, subtly or otherwise, that children are braver, smarter, and more interesting than grown-ups, and that grown-up rules are made to be broken.

Rowling Celebrates Childhood

J.K. (Joanne) Rowling, the Scottish author of the newest British children's classics, the brilliant and phenomenally successful Harry Potter books, is clearly in this tradition. She has created a world in which children have special abilities, while conventional adults are either clueless or cruel or both. Her hero's secret power takes traditional folk-tale forms (flying brooms, transformation, spells and potions). But it can also be seen as a metaphor for the power of childhood: of imagination, of creativity, and of humor (as well as being exciting, her books are often very funny). And like other famous children's authors, Rowling remains close to her own childhood. "I really can, with no difficulty at all, think myself back to eleven years old," she recently told *Time* magazine.

Essentially, the Harry Potter stories belong to an ongoing tradition of Anglo-American fantasy that takes off from [J.R.R.] Tolkien and C.S. Lewis, and has been continued splendidly by writers like [American Newberry Award–winning fantasy author] Lloyd Alexander, [English fantasy author of *The Dark is Rising* series] Susan Cooper, [English fantasy writer] Alan Garner, and [English fantasy writer] Diana Wynne Jones. (Jones's excellent *Charmed Life*, like the Potter books, takes place in a school for juvenile witches and wizards located in an enchanted castle.) What sets Rowling's books apart from their predecessors is partly a lighthearted fertility of invention that recalls L. Frank Baum's Oz books. Even more important is the fact that hers is a fully imagined world, to which she has a deep, ongoing commitment. For six years, even before she began the first book in the series, Rowling was imagining and elaborating its fantasy world. She . . . planned seven Harry Potter novels, one for each year Harry will spend at Hogwarts School of Witchcraft and Wizardry, an institution which seems to be located (like J.K. Rowling herself) somewhere in Scotland.

HARRY AS FOLK HERO

Harry, Rowling's hero, is a natural-born wizard, but at first he doesn't know it. When we meet him he is ten years old and in the classic Cinderlad situation: a poor, lonely orphan, despised and abused. Harry lives with his deeply unpleasant aunt and uncle, Mr. and Mrs. Dursley, in a country that much resembles Britain in the 1960s or 1970s, before the Internet, digital phones, and interactive video.

The Dursleys live in a village called Little Whinging (a joke that American readers may not get: we would call the place Little Whining). Like most of their neighbors, they are Muggles—people who have no magic powers. They hate the very mention of the supernatural, and refuse to give Harry any information about his dead parents. ("They were weirdos, no denying it, and the world's better off without them in my opinion," Uncle Vernon declares.) Uncle Vernon and Aunt Petunia are as cruel to Harry as any fairy-tale stepparent: they feed him poorly and clothe him shabbily; they make him sleep in a dark spider-infested cupboard under the stairs and destroy his mail. Even worse is their son Dudley, a spoiled, overweight, greedy bully who, with the help of his large and hateful friends, makes Harry's school and home life actively miserable.

From the point of view of an imaginative child, the world

is full of Muggles—people who don't understand you, make stupid rules, and want nothing to do with the unexpected or the unseen. Harry's story also embodies the common childhood fantasy that the dreary adults and siblings you live with are not your real family, that you are somehow special and gifted. Harry has an outward manifestation of his gift: a scar in the shape of a lightning bolt on his forehead, the sign that even as a baby he could not be killed by the evil off-stage Dark Wizard Voldemort, whose very name most people fear to utter.

As in many folk tales, you can often tell a character's character from his or her name, and "Voldemort" neatly combines the ideas of theft, mold, and death. Harry Potter, on the other hand, has a name that suggests not only craftsmanship but both English literature and English history: Shakespeare's Prince Hal and Harry Hotspur, the brave, charming, impulsive heroes of *Henry IV*; and Beatrix Potter, who created that other charming and impulsive classic hero, Peter Rabbit.

LIFE AT HOGWARTS

At the start of each story Harry Potter is living in exile at the Dursleys. But presently, with the help of magic, he is rescued and enters an alternate world in which imagination and adventurousness are rewarded. A comic cockney giant named Hagrid introduces him to a parallel magical Britain, one entrance to which is through the back door of a scruffy London pub called the Leaky Cauldron. After a shopping trip in which Harry visits a bank run by goblins and purchases unusual school supplies, including "one plain pointed hat (black) for day wear" and *The Standard Book of Spells (Grade 1)*, he takes a special train to the Hogwarts School of Witchcraft and Wizardry from Track Nine and Three-Quarters at King's Cross Station—a train and track which are, naturally, invisible to Muggles.

Hogwarts School, it turns out, is located in a huge ancient

castle, well-equipped with towers, dungeons, ghosts, secret passages, and enchanted paintings and mirrors. The subjects taught there include Divination, Defense Against the Dark Arts, and Care of Magical Creatures. But in some ways Hogwarts resembles a classic English boarding school—one which, in keeping with the times, is co-ed and multiracial. There are four houses, which compete intensely in the school sport of Quidditch, a sort of combination cricket, soccer, and hockey played on flying broomsticks, in which Harry turns out to excel. The teachers wear black gowns and dine at a head table, and there are prefects and a Head Boy and Head Girl.

Just as in many American schools, however, the student population is roughly divided into jocks, brains, nice guys, and dangerous Goths. Harry and his two best friends are in the jock house, Gryffindor, where, according to tradition, "dwell the brave at heart." Ravenclaw House emphasizes "wit and learning," while the kids in Hufflepuff are described as "just and loyal . . . / And unafraid of toil." The bad characters live in Slytherin House, whose students "use any means/To achieve their ends."

Even before he arrives at Hogwarts, Harry acquires an enemy in Slytherin House, the mean, snobbish, unscrupulous Draco Malfoy, whose name translates readily into "Dragon Bad-Faith." Like Cousin Dudley in the Muggles world, Draco has a couple of goons (these ones are named Crabbe and Goyle) to back up his constant sneering and bullying. As a hero and local sports star, Harry also attracts fans; naturally modest, he finds their intense admiration and constant attention as embarrassing as J.K. Rowling reportedly does.

HARRY VS. EVIL FORCES

But Harry also has more serious problems. The plot of each book essentially centers around the attempts of dark forces to destroy him. As is customary in modern fantasies, from Tolkien's *Lord of the Rings* to *Star Wars*, lurking in the background is an evil, powerful figure (almost always male) who wants to rule the world. Often these characters have something in common with [English author John] Milton's rebel angels [in *Paradise Lost*]: at first they seem impressive and even convincing. There is something admirable in their desire for knowledge and power, whereas their followers, motivated mainly by fear, greed, and revenge, are wholly repulsive.

Harry, of course, always escapes his enemies, but it gets harder with each book. Rowling has said that as time passes the stories will turn darker. "There will be deaths," she has informed *Time* magazine. . . . [I]n volume three it is not so easy to tell which side anyone is on. Those who at first seem friends may be foes, or vice versa; and good but weak people may be seduced into doing evil because of their own fear or folly. In . . . *Harry Potter and the Prisoner of Azkaban*, a scruffy but harmless-looking pet rat called Scabbers turns out to be a wicked wizard who, even in human form, has a "pointed nose and . . . very small, watery eyes."

Rowling describes her characters with a psychological subtlety rare in children's books and sometimes even in adult fiction. In *Harry Potter and the Chamber of Secrets* a ragged, oppressed house-elf named Dobby is constantly torn between loyalty to his masters and his wish to save Harry's life. Whenever he is on the edge of revealing their plots, Dobby hits himself over the head with the nearest blunt object, repeating "Bad Dobby!"

IMPERFECT CHARACTERS

One attraction of the Potter books is that the good characters are not perfect. Harry excels at Quidditch, but he is only an average student, unlike his friend Hermione, who studies for the fun of it and is a bit of a prig. Hagrid, the lovable giant gamekeeper, has a weakness for dangerous magic creatures: he sees his vicious pet dragon and the huge spiders that live in the Forbidden Forest as cute and cuddly. The British, of course, are fanatic animal lovers; and it may be that this is Rowling's comment on some of the peculiar or even dangerous but beloved pets that visitors to England sometimes encounter.

Though Rowling's child heroes are imperfect, they are usually smarter and braver than adults. Some of the nicest teachers at Hogwarts, though friendly and knowledgeable, often don't have a clue to what's going on around them. Others are weak and incompetent, or complete phonies, like the handsome, media-intoxicated Professor Lockhart, who claims to have performed the magical exploits of other, less photogenic wizards. A few, even, may have sold out to the Dark Powers or their representatives.

The headmaster of Hogwarts, elderly silver-haired Professor Dumbledore (like Tolkien's Gandalf, whom he much resembles), maintains a kind of benign detachment from events except in moments of great crisis. A.O. Scott, writing in the on-line magazine *Slate*, has perceptively remarked that "Dumbledore's benevolent but strict theology, involving the operations of free will in a supernaturally determined world, is classically Miltonian."

The appeal of the Harry Potter books, to judge by the flood of reviews and essays that have greeted their appearance, is wide and varied. They can be enjoyed, for instance, as the celebration of a pre-industrial world: Hogwarts Castle is lit by torches and heated by fires, and mail is carried by owls of different sizes, including "tiny little scops owls ('Local Deliveries Only')."

As with most first-rate children's books there is something here for everyone. Pico Iyer, in *The New York Times Book Review*, sees the stories as only half-fantastic accounts of life in an English public school [in England a "public" school is a private one] (in his case Eton [an English boarding school]), "designed to train the elite in a system that other mortals cannot follow." There, as at Hogwarts, he claims, "we were in an alternative reality where none of the usual rules applied." A.O. Scott, on the other hand, thinks that "being a wizard is very much like being gay: you grow up in a hostile world governed by codes and norms that seem nonsensical to you, and you discover at a certain age that there are people like you." (It seems unlikely that Harry Potter is gay: in the [fourth] volume he shows romantic interest in an "extremely pretty" girl Quidditch player called Cho Chang.)

ROWLING FROM RAGS TO RICHES

Joanne Rowling's own story, like Harry's, is in the classic folk-tale tradition. As almost everyone now knows, when she was writing *Harry Potter and the Sorcerer's Stone* she was a young single mother with long red hair, living on public assistance in Edinburgh. Because her flat was unheated, she would put her small daughter into a stroller and push her about the streets until the child fell asleep. Then she would go to a café, order a cup of coffee, and write.

Rowling's fairy godmother was the Scottish Arts Council, which gave her a grant that made it possible for her to finish the first volume. But even then she had trouble getting transportation to the ball. *Harry Potter and the Philosopher's Stone* was rejected by nine English publishers before Bloomsbury took it, and they had no idea it would be such a success. At first they made no special attempt to promote the book, and printed only a small number of copies.

Now, of course, all that is history. [In 1999] the three volumes of the series are number one, two, and three on the *New York Times* best-seller list. (This has annoyed several publishers of adult fiction, who have protested that a children's book really doesn't belong there.) The first volume is being translated into (at last count) twenty-eight languages. A new plaincover edition has also appeared in England, for adults who are embarrassed to be seen reading a children's book. Though this edition costs two pounds more than the original, it has already sold 20,000 copies.

[In 1999] Rowling's publishers have announced that *Harry Potter and the Sorcerer's Stone* will be made into a "live-action" film by Warner Brothers. The script will be written by Steven Kloves, the author and director of *The Fabulous Baker Boys*—a strange choice, some might think. Soon, no doubt, the original book will be edged out of public consciousness by the movie. There will be Harry Potter T-shirts, lunchboxes, video games, and action figures.

There are other looming threats to Harry Potter. In the American South and in Southern California, the same sort of people who object to the teaching of evolution and the Big Bang theory of creation have begun to complain that the stories portray witchcraft in a favorable light. From time to time, of course, the same complaint has been made about the Oz books, which in some cases have been removed from schools and bookstores along with all other representations of cute or friendly wizards and witches. The publishers have not tried to hush this up; from their point of view, any publicity is good publicity.

As a result of all this attention and success, the folk-tale heroine J.K. Rowling, once a welfare mother, has become a fabulously rich princess. Will she now find true love and live happily ever after? Will she be destroyed by the curses of fundamentalist Christians, or fall under the spell of wicked merchandisers and publicists? Her story promises to be almost as interesting as the future adventures of Harry Potter himself.

For Further Research

Works by J.K. Rowling

J.K. Rowling, *Harry Potter and the Chamber of Secrets.* New York: Scholastic, 1999.

————, *Harry Potter and the Goblet of Fire.* New York: Scholastic, 2000.

————, *Harry Potter and the Prisoner of Azkaban.* New York: Scholastic, 1999.

————, *Harry Potter and the Sorcerer's Stone.* New York: Scholastic, 1998. Originally published as *Harry Potter and the Philosopher's Stone.* London: Bloomsbury, 1997.

Newt Scamander, *Fantastic Beasts and Where to Find Them.* New York: Scholastic, 2001.

Kennilworthy Whisp, *Quidditch Through the Ages.* New York: Scholastic, 2001.

Books About J.K. Rowling and *Harry Potter*

David Colbert, *The Magical Worlds of Harry Potter.* Wrightsville Beach, NC: Lumina Press, 2001.

Lindsey Fraser, *Conversations with J.K. Rowling.* New York: Scholastic, 2000.

Allan Zola Kronzek and Elizabeth Kronzek, *The Sorcerer's Companion.* New York: Broadway Books, 2001.

Connie Neal, *What's a Christian to Do with Harry Potter?* Colorado Springs, CO: WaterBrook Press, 2001.

Philip Nel, *J.K. Rowling's Harry Potter Novels: A Reader's Guide.* New York: Continuum International, 2001.

Elizabeth D. Schafer, *Exploring Harry Potter.* Osprey, FL: Beacham, 2000.

Marc Shapiro, *J.K. Rowling: The Wizard Behind Harry Potter.* New York: St. Martin's Griffin, 2000.

Sean Smith, *J.K. Rowling: A Biography.* London: Michael O'Mara, 2001.

Index